From

Word

To

Work

From **Word** *To* **Work**

Walking the Spiritual Workflow of God

Joshua Watson

Published by Meadow Elk Publishing | Houston, Texas

ISBN 979-8-90403-000-1 (paperback)
ISBN 979-8-90403-001-8 (hardcover)
ISBN 979-8-90403-002-5 (ebook)
Library of Congress Control Number: 2026936882
Cataloging-in-Publication data is available from the Library of Congress.

First Edition, 2026

Cover design by Ayo Balogun-Emanuel
Interior design and layout by Ayo Balogun-Emanuel

For permissions, inquiries, or ministry correspondence:
info@meadowelkpublishing.com
www.meadowelkpublishing.com

Printed in the United States of America

Acknowledgments

First, I give all honor to God my Father, whose love, wisdom, and unchanging faithfulness sustained every step of this journey.

To the Lord Jesus Christ, my Savior and Shepherd, whose Word is the foundation of every truth written in these pages.

And to the Holy Spirit, my Teacher, my Guide, and my Helper, thank You for revelation, conviction, and comfort. Every insight, every correction, and every spark of clarity came from Your gentle voice. Anything good in this work is the fruit of Your presence.

To my wife, whose strength and grace reflect the beauty of the woman in Proverbs 31. You have been my encourager, my steady place, and my closest companion in the things of God. You have supported me, challenged me, prayed over me, and believed in me long before these words were written. This book carries your fingerprints as much as mine. Your courage has empowered me, your wisdom has sharpened me, and your love has sustained me. I am forever grateful to you.

To my dear friend and theological editor, Reilly Douglass, thank you for being a prayer warrior, a confidant, and a role model. Your insight, discernment, and devotion to the truth of Scripture strengthened every chapter. Your friendship is a gift, and your faithfulness to God's Word is a steady encouragement.

And finally, to every reader who opens these pages with a desire to walk more closely with God.

May the same Spirit who led me through this writing lead you through every season of obedience, and may His voice become the most familiar sound in your life.

Introduction

There comes a point in every believer's life when hearing God's Word is no longer enough. We read, we listen, we underline verses, but something inside us longs for more than information. We want transformation. We want to walk in what we know, not simply admire it from a distance. We want to see God's promises move from the pages of Scripture into the soil of our daily lives.

This book was born out of that longing.

Many of us have been taught to love the Word, but not all of us have been taught how to work the Word, how to cooperate with God in the everyday process of spiritual growth. Scripture reveals repeatedly that God plants, speaks, and forms before He manifests anything. His work in us follows the same pattern. Faith begins as a seed. It develops roots. It grows in hidden places. And then, in time, it bears fruit that can be seen.

But between the Word and the fruit, there is a journey. It is the journey from revelation to obedience, from hearing to doing, from believing to becoming. It is the movement from promise to participation, from inspiration to endurance. And that journey is where many believers grow weary, confused, or stuck. Some wait for God to finish what He already instructed them to begin. Others start well but lose heart when the process becomes slow, quiet, or costly. Still others cherish the truths of scripture but never see those truths transform their homes, their speech, their habits, or their inner life.

This book was written for every believer who has ever asked:

"Why does the distance between God's promise and my reality feel so wide?"

"What has God already done, and what is He waiting for me to obey?"

"How do I take what God has spoken and walk it out faithfully?"

In these chapters, you will walk through the spiritual journey God designed for every one of His children. Through the story of Elias and his family, you will see how the Word of God takes root in the human heart, how faith matures through trials, how obedience strengthens the soul, and how God turns ordinary actions into holy partnerships. You will see that spiritual formation is not mystical or unreachable, but deeply practical. God meets you in the words you speak, the steps you take, the habits you form, and the choices you repeat.

Each chapter will guide you through a pattern found throughout Scripture. God plants His Word and revelation begins something in the heart. Faith either rises or fear resists as the heart responds. The mouth aligns as words create atmosphere and direction. Obedience moves, making faith visible through action. Endurance strengthens as consistency turns faith into character. Fruit appears, and what God started becomes what others can see.

This is the rhythm of the Kingdom. This is the process by which God transforms every life surrendered to Him. As you move through this book, you will find both story and Scripture weaving together, teaching not only principles but patterns, living examples of how God works in those who trust Him.

The transformation you can expect is not a sudden burst of inspiration but a steady reordering of your inner world. Your speech will change first, then your choices, then your habits, then the atmosphere of your home, and finally the legacy you leave behind. This is not self-help. This is surrender. This is cooperation with the Spirit of God, who works in us "both to will and to do of His good pleasure."

My prayer is that these pages lead you into a deeper confidence, not in your own ability, but in the faithful God who watches over His Word to perform it. May you discover that the same God who speaks the seed also supplies the strength to grow it. And may you learn, step by step, how to move from Word to Work until your life becomes the very testimony He intends it to be.

Now, let us begin the journey.

PART I

The Soil and the Seed: Preparing for the Word

God's Word begins as a seed, just as Jesus taught when He described a farmer scattering seed across different kinds of soil. Some soil was hard, some was shallow, some was crowded, and some was prepared. The seed was always the same, but the outcome depended on the condition of the soil it was planted in. In the same way, our hearts become the place where God's Word either takes root or withers before it can grow.

In this section, we'll learn what it means to meditate on God's Word until it becomes alive inside of us, not merely memorized, but experienced.

Through the story of The Shepherd's Path and the lessons that follow, we'll discover how to prepare our hearts for lasting growth.

Chapter 1

The Shepherd's Path

"The Lord is my shepherd; I shall not want."
(Psalm 23:1, KJV)

The first loss was money, but the wound reached deeper than empty pockets. Elias had always been diligent, a young shepherd with a modest flock and a strip of land his father once called faithful soil. So when the traveling merchant arrived with tidy ledgers, fine promises, and a voice smooth as oil, Elias saw what looked like opportunity: shared pasture rights, expanded routes, buyers in distant towns. The contract was clean. The seal looked official. The words sounded like rain to dry ground.

By season's end, the merchant was gone. The seals proved to be wax without weight, and the merchant's team had driven off the livestock Elias pledged in the agreement through a trail of dust. Some neighbors pitied him from their doorways. Others whispered behind their hands. "Too trusting," some said. "Too soft," said others.

Elias said nothing. Something inside him had gone silent. He walked the boundary of his fields at dusk, boots crunching over brittle earth. The fenceposts leaned like tired older men. The lambing shelter sagged where years of sun had eaten through the boards. Once, he had been a builder. Now he was merely a witness to ruin.

The thief had come to steal. The thief had succeeded.

That night, he lay down in the open, too weary to return to the house. The ground was cold beneath his spine, the sky dim and indifferent above him. He had once believed the heavens told a story. Now they seemed only distant.

"Lord," he whispered, voice ragged, "You see... but do You speak?"

No answer came but the wind.

He pulled his cloak over his shoulders and stared into the starlit emptiness. He tried to pray, tried to say the words that used to anchor him.

"The Lord is my shepherd, I shall not want." The words broke in his throat, hollow and unbelievable. Shame warmed his cheeks more than the cloak.

His thoughts spiraled, doubt and confusion and pain, until sleep rose over him like deep water, pulling him downward until the waking world dissolved.

Elias opened his eyes, though he did not know he was dreaming.

The world around him shimmered, too vivid for waking and too grounded for imagination. He stood in a wilderness of fractured color. Yellow grass bowed under a restless wind. Gray stones jutted from the ground like long-forgotten bones. Above him hung a white sun, radiating heat without comfort.

A scent of cedar drifted through the dry air, carrying something older, something familiar, as a half-remembered memory.

Ahead, on a rise of rock, stood a Figure.

Not a mirage. Not a trick of heat. No blur and no shimmer. Only presence.

His robe was plain and travel-worn. His posture was steady. His eyes, calm flame and deep water at once, held Elias with a gentleness that felt like truth made visible.

"Walk with Me," the Stranger said.

Elias hesitated. He had walked with promises before and found only lies. Yet something in the Stranger's voice, the quiet authority and the stillness within it, moved past his caution. He nodded and fell into step beside Him.

> *"The Lord is my shepherd; I shall not want."*
> (Psalm 23:1, KJV)

They walked without hurry. The ground beneath their feet shifted from pale clay to soil that remembered rain. The air cooled. Greenery rose faintly around them.

The Stranger stopped beside a valley where grass grew thick and soft. Water whispered nearby over hidden stones.

> *"He maketh me to lie down in green pastures. He leadeth me beside the still waters."*
> (Psalm 23:2, KJV)

Elias knelt, breath catching. The grass held him like a bed fashioned by peace itself. He crawled to the stream and cupped his hands. The water shocked him with cold at the first sip, then flooded his insides with rest. Tears surprised him. He did not wipe them away.

"You asked me to speak," the Stranger said, "but your heart carried no room for My words."

Elias bowed his head. "I have nothing left."

"You have Me," the Stranger replied, and the words settled over Elias like cool shade at noon.

They rose and continued along a narrow path that wove between low hills scattered with wild olive trees. It carried them forward with intention, steady and sure beneath their feet, guiding them exactly where they were meant to go.

"He restoreth my soul: He leadeth me in the paths of righteousness for his name's sake."
(Psalm 23:3, KJV)

"Why this way?" Elias asked as the path tightened into a stony corridor.

"Because it is the right way," the Stranger said. "Not the easy way, but the right way."

The corridor narrowed further, shadow swallowing the light as Elias followed close behind the Stranger. Low echoes of old accusations filled the air. "You were foolish. You trusted the wrong hands. You are alone here." Shapes shifted at the edge of his vision, teeth and claws and threat pressing in from the dark.

His pulse kicked. Elias reached out, pressing a trembling hand to the cold stone wall. "I cannot see you," he said, breath quickening, his eyes straining ahead.

"You do not need to see Me," the Stranger answered, His voice steady and near, as if spoken just over Elias's shoulder. "You need only to know that I am with you."

Then a soft glow rose from the staff in the Stranger's hand, illuminating the path just enough to see the next step. The shadows shrank back, as though the light had blunted their teeth. With each step Elias took, his fear loosened its grip.

"Yea, though I walk through the valley of the shadow of death, I will fear no evil: for thou art with me; Thy rod and thy staff they comfort me."
(Psalm 23:4, KJV)

The path opened suddenly into a sun-washed clearing. At the center stood a polished, beautiful table. Loaves steamed with warmth. Fruit glistened as if lit from within. A cup sat filled to the brim.

Figures stood at the edges of the light, faces he recognized. The merchant. The neighbors who whispered. His younger self. They watched from the shadows but could not cross into the circle of radiance.

The Stranger motioned to the table. Elias sat. The bread soothed the ache behind his ribs. The fruit tasted like a harvest after drought. The cup overflowed as if the table insisted he drink more than he believed he deserved.

Warm oil touched his head, fragrant with cedar and myrrh and something heavenly, running down to his jaw and washing away years of unspoken wounds.

"Thou preparest a table before me in the presence of mine enemies: Thou anointest my head with oil; my cup runneth over."
(Psalm 23:5, KJV)

They rose again and walked toward a horizon rimmed with gold. Two figures followed behind, one radiant and one heavy with kindness.

"What are their names?" Elias asked.

"Goodness," the Stranger said, nodding to the first, "and Mercy," nodding to the second. "They follow you always, even when you do not see them."

The valley widened. In the distance stood a house unlike any Elias had known, yet deeply familiar, like home remembered rather than discovered.

"Surely goodness and mercy shall follow me all the days of my life: And I will dwell in the house of the Lord for ever."
(Psalm 23:6, KJV)

They stopped. The Stranger turned so Elias could see His face clearly. Kindness and authority lived there together without tension.

"Elias," He said, and hearing his name in that voice stitched together something the thief had torn.

"Rise. Tend what I give you. Prepare the ground. I will be with you in the field and in the furrow, in the word and in the work."

"But how?" Elias asked, part plea and part prayer.

"As I have shown you," the Stranger said. "Rest before striving. Follow before forcing. Fear no evil in narrow places. Eat what I prepare, even when opposition watches. Let oil mark you as Mine. Walk with goodness and mercy behind you. And dwell with Me even in open places that look like loss."

Light rose around them, bright and warm and consuming.

Elias reached for it...

And woke.

Dawn had not yet broken, but the eastern sky glowed faintly. The field lay unchanged, the fence leaning and the soil cracked, yet nothing was the same.

He sat up slowly, the cold earth on his back and the warmth of the dream in his chest. He touched his hair, half expecting oil to cling to his fingertips. Only memory remained, a memory too real to dismiss.

He stood and walked the boundary of his land. Frost had begun to melt under a thin breath of wind. He knelt and pressed his fingers into the soil. The first inch was stubborn, but the second gave way as if remembering softness.

"The Lord is my shepherd," he whispered. This time, the words did not taste like dust. They tasted like bread.

He rose and turned toward the barn. The old plow leaned against the wall as if waiting faithfully for its return.

Elias set his shoulder to the beam, and the ground finally yielded.

Behind him, though he could not hear them, two presences followed with the patience of seasons.

Goodness.

Mercy.

Seeing Scripture Come Alive

Many believers approach the Bible as though it were a textbook, something to study, underline, memorize, or recite correctly. Yet when real life presses in, the very truths they highlighted often fade. Peace slips away in the moment they need it most. Fear returns louder than the promises they once read with excitement. The reason is simple: the Word was never meant to live only in the intellect. It was designed to root itself in the heart and bear fruit through experience.

Scripture describes this shallow encounter with striking accuracy:

"For if any be a hearer of the word, and not a doer, he is like unto a man beholding his natural face in a glass: For he beholdeth himself, and goeth his way, and straightway forgetteth what manner of man he was."
(James 1:23-24, KJV)

A person may remember the Word for a moment, just as one remembers a reflection in a mirror, yet walk away unchanged. Reading without revelation is like glancing at your face but never washing it. The Word reveals what must change, but only when we engage it with faith, imagination, and obedience does it begin to cleanse and transform us.

To truly "see" Scripture is to treat it as a living conversation rather than ancient speech frozen on a page. Every verse is the breath of God preserved for today. His Word was not given merely for education but for participation. The Spirit of God still hovers over every verse, just as He hovered over the waters in Genesis, waiting for believers to speak light into their own chaos.

When the heart begins to interact with the Word, when you ponder it, picture it, and respond to it, the printed text becomes a living voice within the soul.

Psalm 23 is a perfect example. It is not a distant poem about a shepherd in the past. It is a divine portrait of how God personally leads His people through every season. When you allow Scripture to form scenes in your imagination, you are not creating fantasy. You are cooperating with the Holy Spirit, who often communicates truth through the language of vision. The God who gave Joseph dreams and Ezekiel visions still uses sanctified imagination to write truth upon the heart.

This is the biblical art of meditation. It is the practice of turning written truth into an inner landscape where the Spirit can walk with you. In that sacred space, verses become pathways and promises become rooms filled with light. Biblical meditation allows the eternal Word to clothe itself in the language of your life so that what you see in Scripture becomes what you live in reality.

This inner cultivation is what Scripture calls the renewing of the mind:

"And be not conformed to this world: but be ye transformed by the renewing of your mind, that ye may prove what is that good, and acceptable, and perfect, will of God."
(Romans 12:2, KJV)

Transformation begins in the imagination. As a man thinks in his heart, so is he. What the heart continually beholds, it becomes. When you picture the truths of Scripture, you train your inner life to think heaven's thoughts. The renewed mind is not empty; it is a mind filled with images of God's faithfulness and promises, shaped by the Word until thinking and believing align with His nature.

Unlike the world's meditation, which empties the mind and focuses on self, biblical meditation fills the mind with God's voice until every competing sound grows still. It is not the absence of thought, but the presence of truth. To meditate biblically is to linger in the Word long enough that it begins to speak back. You hold each verse like a seed, turning it over in your heart until it releases its life.

The prophet Jeremiah described this experience vividly:

"Thy words were found, and I did eat them; and thy word was unto me the joy and rejoicing of mine heart:"
(Jeremiah 15:16, KJV)

Jeremiah did not simply read the Word; he consumed it. He let it nourish him. This is spiritual digestion. You take the words in slowly, savoring their meaning, until they become part of you.

This is why Scripture frequently describes the Word as seed. Seed must enter good soil, rest unseen, break open, and then rise. The hidden breaking comes first, the transformation that no one sees. It happens in the heart when the believer allows the Spirit to apply the Word personally.

Jesus taught:

"Now the parable is this: The seed is the word of God."
(Luke 8:11, KJV)

Jesus went on to explain that the seed is always the same, but the soil is not. Some hearts are hardened, some shallow, some crowded, and some prepared, and the condition of the soil determines whether the Word takes root and bears fruit. Meditation prepares the heart as soil, and faith as warmth, creating the conditions for the seed to germinate and grow.

As you meditate on Scripture, you begin to sense the voice of the Holy Spirit guiding your understanding. He brings verses to memory with perfect timing, weaving the Word into your thoughts. Jesus promised this ministry plainly:

"But the Comforter, which is the Holy Ghost, whom the Father will send in my name, he shall teach you all things, and bring all things to your remembrance, whatsoever I have said unto you."
(John 14:26, KJV)

The Spirit does not shout over you. He whispers truth with a peace that signals His presence. As you cultivate stillness in meditation, you learn to distinguish His voice from your own thoughts. He becomes the Shepherd who leads your inner life beside still waters.

The traveler in the story did not rush through Psalm 23. He lived it. He walked its valleys and drank from its promises.

Provision. "I shall not want." God supplies what is needed for every step.

Peace. "He makes me lie down." Before God teaches progress, He teaches rest.

Guidance. "He leads me." The path of righteousness is discovered through following, not forcing.

Protection. "Your rod and staff comfort me." Correction is not punishment, it is love with direction.

Purpose. "You prepare a table." God sets victory before His children, even in the presence of opposition.

Presence. "I will dwell." Every path ends in abiding communion with Him.

When Scripture becomes a landscape you enter rather than a line you read, you stop reading to finish a chapter and begin reading to encounter a Person. That encounter plants the seed deep enough to endure.

How To Meditate on the Word

Slow Down the Reading:
Open the passage and read it aloud, phrase by phrase. Let the words breathe. Reading slowly allows your heart to catch up with

your eyes. When your thoughts drift, gently pull them back. This is how the mind is renewed, as Romans 12:2 teaches.

Engage Your Imagination:

Picture the verse as if you were standing inside it. If the Scripture speaks of still waters, imagine the sound and scent of peace. Your imagination is not an enemy to Scripture; it is a tool that God sanctifies for faith.

Personalize It:

Replace the pronouns with your name. "The Lord is Joshua's shepherd." Speaking in this way builds ownership and agreement.

Listen for the Spirit:

After reading, be still. Ask, "Lord, what are You showing me today?" The Holy Spirit will highlight specific phrases or bring understanding to your present circumstances.

Record the Revelation:

Write what you sense. Journaling moves truth from invisible impression to visible form and becomes a record of God's guidance.

Pray the Word Back:

Turn the verse into a prayer. "Lord, restore my soul today. Lead me in peace." This anchors the Word into your daily walk.

Meditation is not mystical or complicated. It is simply intentional lingering. The more you practice, the quicker you recognize the Shepherd's voice and the more easily you rest in His truth. Day by day, your mind becomes renewed, and the heart becomes fertile soil where the Word can take root and bear fruit.

Before moving forward, pause to let the seed of this chapter settle. The goal is not information, but transformation. Take a moment to breathe, to listen, and to let the Shepherd speak to you personally through His Word.

Reflection & Practice

1. Reflection
Sit with the following questions slowly without rushing to "get the right answer."

Do I approach Scripture as information to consume, or as a place to encounter God?

What shifts in me when I expect the Holy Spirit to meet me in the Word?

Let your heart respond before your intellect attempts to explain.

2. Scripture Meditation

"Open thou mine eyes, That I may behold wondrous things out of thy law."
(Psalm 119:18, KJV)

Read it aloud. Reread it, slower. Ask the Holy Spirit to make this more than a verse. Let it become your prayer for illumination.

3. Prayer of Alignment
Lord, open my eyes to Your Word. Let Scripture become more than ink on a page. Let it become a place where I encounter You. Teach me to linger long enough for truth to take root. Sanctify my imagination so that every verse becomes a doorway into Your presence. Let Your Spirit bring light, clarity, conviction, and renewal. Transform the landscape of my thoughts through Your living Word. Train my heart to hear Your voice, follow Your leading, and walk with You through every line of Scripture. In Jesus' name, amen.

4. Action Step
Choose one passage that is short, simple, and familiar.

Examples: Psalm 23, Psalm 1, John 10:1-10, Romans 8:1-4

Today, enter the Scripture instead of studying around it:

Read it aloud.

Imagine the scene as though you are standing inside it.

Ask the Holy Spirit, "What are You showing me here?"

Write one sentence beginning with:

"The Lord revealed…" or "The Lord highlighted…"

This single sentence is your first seed in the soil of a mind that is being renewed.

5. Practice for the Week
For the next seven days, stay with the same passage. Let God work in the repetition.

Daily practice:

Read the passage morning and night.

After each reading, please close your eyes and visualize its truth.

Speak the Scripture aloud in the first person:

> *"The Lord is my shepherd; I shall not want."*
> (Psalm 23:1, KJV)

Record one short observation in a journal. Do not aim for perfection or depth; write what stood out to you. It may be a word, a phrase, a feeling, or a moment of clarity. This is not about analyzing yourself, but about noticing what the Spirit is drawing your attention to. Over time, these small observations become markers of growth and guidance. What you record today may become the insight God reminds you of tomorrow.

Close with a simple prayer:" Lord, root this Word in me."

By the end of the week, you will notice the early signs of renewal, a quieting of the inner world, a sharper awareness of the Spirit, and a sense that Scripture is no longer a page but a meeting place.

This is how the Word begins to take root. This is how a renewed mind begins to form.

Closing Prayer

"Father, thank You for being my Shepherd. Teach me to see Your Word until I can walk it out with confidence. Break the hard soil of distraction; plant Your truth deep in me. Let still waters saturate my thoughts and emotions. Restore my soul and renew my mind until it mirrors the mind of Christ. Lead me on the path that brings You glory. In Jesus' name, Amen."

Chapter 2

The Dream of the Shepherd King

"Sow to yourselves in righteousness, Reap in mercy; Break up your fallow ground: For it is time to seek the Lord, Till he come and rain righteousness upon you."
(Hosea 10:12, KJV)

Sleep faded slowly, and Elias woke before dawn. The world was still hushed, wrapped in the pale blue light before morning. Something inside him had changed. The dream was not fading as dreams usually do; it remained, settling deep within him like truth spoken by God.

He rose slowly, brushing the chill of night from his cloak, and walked toward the edge of the field. The frost glimmered faintly beneath his feet, yet the ground felt softer than the day before, almost as if the soil itself remembered the footsteps of the Stranger.

Elias knelt and placed his hand flat against the earth. "Restore my soul," he whispered, barely hearing his own voice.

A breeze stirred the grass. Warmth moved through him, subtle yet undeniable, as though heaven was answering without sound.

As the sun climbed, Elias returned to the house. His wife, Hannah, was already at the hearth, grinding barley and humming the melody of an old psalm. She looked up as he entered, concern flickering across her face.

"You were gone long this morning," she said gently.

He paused by the door, still halfway between worlds. "I had a dream," he said. "But it was more than a dream. I met someone."

Hannah's hands stilled. She studied his expression the way she used to study the sky before storms. "Tell me."

He recounted the valley, the paths, the shadows, the table, and the anointing oil. He told her of the Shepherd's voice and the words that had undone him and remade him at once. Hannah listened without interruption, her eyes widening only when he spoke of goodness and mercy following him like living companions.

When he finished, she released a long breath. "Elias, this was not your imagination. This was a visitation."

He nodded. "I know."

"You heard His voice."

"I did."

She stepped toward him, resting a hand on his arm. "Then what will you do with what He said?"

Elias looked past her toward the fields. "He told me to tend what He gives me. But the fields are worn. The plow is old. I am not sure where to begin."

Hannah smiled softly. "Begin where He met you. Begin in the valley of the shadow. Walk through your fear, and you will find the path."

Her words settled into him like a seed. He knew she was right. The dream had not come solely to comfort him; it had come to awaken him.

Later that morning, Elias took the plow from the barn and inspected it carefully. The handle was weathered, worn by his father's hands and his own. The blade was dull; the wood cracked in places. Yet it felt like it still had a purpose when he lifted it.

He carried it into the fields and set the blade into the soil. His first push barely cut the ground. The earth resisted him. Sweat formed at the base of his neck. He braced himself and pushed again.

This time, the soil gave way.

A line of overturned earth stretched behind him, dark and rich. Elias paused, his breath steadying. A quiet reverence rose in him.

"Yea, though I walk through the valley of the shadow of death," he whispered, "Thou art with me."

Each push of the plow was a prayer. Each footstep carried the memory of the Stranger's voice.

By midday, Hannah came with water and a cloth. She watched the field taking shape. "This is new," she said quietly.

"No," Elias replied. "This is old. This is returning."

She smiled. "Then let us return together."

They spent the rest of the afternoon clearing stones, marking rows, and gathering tools. The boys joined them after their chores, curious at first, then energized by the sight of their father working as if led by a wind they could not see.

"Father," Micah asked, "what changed?"

Elias paused, leaning on the plow. He looked toward the hills where the valley he had seen in his dream once stretched before him. "I remembered who my Shepherd is," he said. "And I remembered I am responsible for what He has placed in my care."

That evening, after the sun dipped behind the hills, Elias walked alone to the fig tree at the vineyard's edge. Fireflies danced among the branches, and the field lay stretched out before him like a promise.

He remembered the table in the dream, the cup overflowing, the oil running down his head. A warmth spread through him, slow and steady, the way peace grows when rooted deep.

"Surely goodness and mercy shall follow me," he said into the quiet air, "all the days of my life."

The words did not fall to the ground. They lingered, hanging in the twilight as if the valley itself remembered them, the way a field remembers rain.

Elias lifted the plow again and set it beside the tree. Tomorrow he would continue the work. Tomorrow, he would walk the land with new eyes.

But tonight, he whispered into the coming dark:

"I shall dwell in Your house, Lord, even as I walk this one."

And for the first time since his loss, he slept without fear.

Breaking Up the Fallow Ground

"Sow to yourselves in righteousness, Reap in mercy; Break up your fallow ground: For it is time to seek the Lord, Till he come and rain righteousness upon you."
(Hosea 10:12, KJV)

Elias's hands on the plow mirror what God desires to do in every believer's heart. Before the seed can take root, the ground must be broken. Before the Word can transform, the heart must be opened.

Many Christians approach Scripture only with the mind. They study, memorize, and quote verses, yet parts of their lives remain unchanged. When truth never penetrates the heart, it becomes like a seed scattered on a hard path. It lies exposed until the enemy steals it.

God's Word is not intended to rest on the surface of the intellect. It is a living seed that must sink into the soil of inner life. Reading for information may fill the head, but reading for revelation breaks the ground of the heart.

How Hearts Become Hard

Hard soil does not form in a single day, and neither does a hard heart. It develops slowly, layer by layer.

It begins with disappointments that are never brought to God. Convictions are brushed aside rather than obeyed. Promptings from the Spirit are delayed "until later." Over time, convenience quietly replaces communion.

Each moment of resistance compresses the soil. Over time, what was once tender becomes compacted and resistant to the very rain we pray for.

The Lord's command to "break up your fallow ground" is not harsh. It is merciful. He is not saying, "I am finished with you." He is saying, "I am ready to plant more in you, but the ground must be turned again."

The prophet Jeremiah echoes this call:

"...Break up your fallow ground, and sow not among thorns."
(Jeremiah 4:3, KJV)

God does not plant on pavement. He waits for a partnership. He waits for the sound of surrender, the turning of the soil.

Hearing That Softens the Heart

"Wherefore (as the Holy Ghost saith, To day if ye will hear his voice, Harden not your hearts, ..."
(Hebrews 3:7-8, KJV)

Before God sows new seed, He restores hearing. A hard heart still hears sound, but not substance. It catches the words of Scripture, but misses the Person speaking through them.

Like Paul says in Romans:

"So then faith cometh by hearing, and hearing by the word of God."
(Romans 10:17, KJV)

Notice that hearing is mentioned twice. There is the hearing of the ear and the hearing of the heart. One receives syllables, the other receives revelation. One fills the mind, the other feeds faith.

True hearing is more than listening. It is yielding.

The Israelites heard the thunder at Sinai, but only Moses drew near. The voice was the same, but the heart responses were different. A soft heart says,

> *"...Speak; for thy servant heareth."*
> (1 Samuel 3:10, KJV)

A hard heart says, "Not now," even if the mouth says "Amen."

Listening with surrender is spiritual tilling. Every time you slow down with the Word, refuse to rush, and ask, "Lord, what are You saying to me in this?", you are turning over the ground of your heart. You are telling God, "I want Your voice to go deeper than my habits."

Choosing What You Hear

If faith comes by hearing, unbelief also comes by hearing, but from different sources. Jesus said.

> *"...Take heed what ye hear:"*
> (Mark 4:24, KJV)

Modern life is loud. News, opinions, fear, arguments, music, entertainment, social media, all compete for the same space your heart needs for the Word. What continually fills your ears will eventually shape your inner soil.

Some voices plant peace. Others plant worry, compromise, or courage.

Ask the Holy Spirit to curate your hearing. He will show you which voices to turn down and which to turn up. Fill your environment with Scripture read aloud, worship that exalts Jesus, and conversations that strengthen faith. These sounds soften the ground. They prepare the heart for the seed.

Diagnosing the Soil

Jesus did not leave us guessing about the condition of our inner field. He told a parable of a sower whose seed fell on four different kinds of soil: the wayside, stony ground, thorny ground, and good ground. The seed was the same in every case, but the outcome depended entirely on the soil it was planted in.

> *"The sower soweth the word. And these are they by the way side, where the word is sown; but when they have heard, Satan cometh immediately, and taketh away the word that was sown in their hearts. And these are they likewise which are sown on stony ground; who, when they have heard the word, immediately receive it with gladness; And have no root in themselves, and so endure but for a time: afterward, when affliction or persecution ariseth for the word's sake, immediately they are offended. And these are they which are sown among thorns; such as hear the word, And the cares of this world, and the deceitfulness of riches, and the lusts of other things entering in, choke the word, and it becometh unfruitful. And these are they which are sown on good ground; such as hear the word, and receive it, and bring forth fruit, some thirtyfold, some sixty, and some an hundred."*
> (Mark 4:14-20, KJV)

Jesus described four soils, not to lock us into a category, but to reveal what is continuously happening inside us. The condition of the soil can change, and Scripture invites us to tend it with honesty and humility. What matters is not where we have been, but whether we are willing to respond to what God is showing us now.

1. The Way-Side Heart: Distracted and Trampled

This heart hears the Word, then immediately loses it. Life passes over it so fast that truth never sinks in. The enemy does not have to work hard here. He only needs a distraction.

If you find that sermons fade by lunchtime and devotions vanish by afternoon, your soil may be near the way side. The remedy is not effort, but stillness. Create space for the Word to land. Linger after you read. Let a single verse stay with you through the day.

"Be still, and know that I am God:"
(Psalm 46:10, KJV)

Stillness is how trampling stops, and the top layer of the heart begins to loosen.

2. The Stony Heart Shallow but Excited

This heart receives the Word quickly "with gladness," but has "no root." There is emotion, but not endurance. Under the surface lie stones that block depth, unresolved pain, pride, or self-protection.

When pressure or persecution comes "for the word's sake," offense rises. The person wonders, "Why is this happening if I believed?" and quietly lets go of what God said.

The only way this soil changes is by allowing God to dig deeper than surface belief. Ask Him, "Show me what hard places in my heart are keeping Your Word from sinking in." These stones may be unhealed wounds, misplaced priorities, hidden fears, or beliefs shaped more by past pain than present truth. When He brings them to light, agree with Him without delay and release them into His care. Each surrendered stone makes room for deeper roots, where faith can endure and grow strong.

3. The Thorn-Filled Heart Crowded and Divided

Here, the seed does grow, but it has competition. Jesus said the Word is choked by "the cares of this world, and the deceitfulness of riches, and the lusts of other things."

This is the believer who sincerely loves God, yet allows worry, ambition, or desire to claim equal space in the heart. The result is that nothing bears whole fruit.

The answer is not to abandon responsibility, but to reorder affection. Ask God, "What cares have grown louder than Your voice in me?" Then begin to surrender them, one by one. Each act of trusting God with a concern is like pulling up a thorn so that the plant of the Word can breathe again.

4. The Good Ground yielded and guarded

Good soil is not naturally superior. It is simply soil that has been broken, cleared, and guarded. This heart "hears the word, and receives it, and brings forth fruit." It welcomes conviction, responds quickly, and protects what God has planted.

Good ground is not perfect ground. It is repentant ground.

This soil is made by cooperation with the Spirit. Every time you say "yes" to His correction, every time you respond rather than resist, a new furrow is turned. Over time, the heart that once resisted becomes the heart that bears thirty, sixty, and one hundred-fold.

Guarding the Field

"Keep thy heart with all diligence; For out of it are the issues of life"
(Proverbs 4:23, KJV)

Once the soil has been broken, it must be maintained. No farmer plows once and then abandons his field. Weeds grow fastest in neglected places, not in fields that are carefully tended.

In the same way, guarding the heart is an ongoing assignment, and Scripture gives us the pattern.

"This book of the law shall not depart out of thy mouth; but thou shalt meditate therein day and night, that thou mayest observe to do according to all that is written therein: for then thou shalt make thy way prosperous, and then thou shalt have good success."
(Joshua 1:8, KJV)

Notice the order. The Word in the mouth. Meditation in the heart. Obedience in life. Fruit in the journey.

Godly meditation keeps the soil moist. Obedience keeps it open. Watchfulness keeps it clean. When these disciplines are neglected, hardness slowly returns.

The good news is that God is patient with His fields. The moment you realize an area has grown hard again, you can return to Hosea's invitation: "Break up your fallow ground, for it is time to seek the Lord." He is always ready to plow where you are willing to yield.

Reflection & Practice

1. Reflection

Ask yourself slowly and honestly: If my heart is a field, which parts are soft and responsive to God, and which parts have quietly become hard, distracted, or crowded? Where have my actions been saying, "Not now, Lord," even when my mouth still says, "Amen"? Invite the Holy Spirit to speak with clarity. Do not rush. Permit Him to show you the actual condition of the soil in your heart. Let your attention rest in His presence until you sense where He is gently directing you.

2. Scripture Meditation

Read this verse aloud, pausing after each phrase. Let the words settle instead of rushing through them. Notice which phrases draw your attention or stir your heart:

"Sow to yourselves in righteousness, Reap in mercy; Break up your fallow ground: For it is time to seek the Lord, Till he come and rain righteousness upon you."
(Hosea 10:12, KJV)

Then read this companion warning and invitation:

"...To day if ye will hear his voice, harden not your hearts"
(Hebrews 3:15, KJV)

Hold these two truths together: It is time to seek the Lord. Do not harden your heart. Sit quietly and let these words move from reading to recognition.

3. Prayer of Alignment

Lord, I bring You the field of my heart. Where I have grown hard through disappointment, delay, sin, or distraction, break up my fallow ground. Reveal the places where I have resisted Your voice or allowed other cares to rise higher than Your Word. I invite You to plow again. Make my heart good soil—soft to Your correction and quick to repent. Teach me to hear with the heart and not only with the ear. Let Your Word sink deeply into my heart, take root, and bear lasting fruit in me. In Jesus' name, amen.

4. Action Step

Diagnose the soil of your heart with God, not by guessing. Today, set aside at least 15-20 quiet minutes.

Read Mark 4:14-20 slowly.

On a blank page, write four headings: Wayside, Stony, Thorn-filled, and good ground.

Under each heading, ask the Holy Spirit: "Where do You see this in me right now?"

Wayside: Where do I hear the truth but forget it quickly?

Stony: Where do I begin well, but withdraw under pressure?

Thorn-filled: Where are worries or distractions choking what You have begun?

Good ground: Where am I receiving, guarding, and yielding fully to Your Word?

Write honestly. Do not argue with what He reveals. Circle one specific area that you sense He is inviting you to break up first. This becomes your next step with Him.

5. Practice for the Week

For the next seven days, tend the same circled area with intention.

Morning: Water the Seed. Read Hosea 10:12 and Proverbs 4:23 aloud. Ask, "Lord, how can I guard my heart in this area today?" Write one clear intention for the day.

Afternoon: Take Heed to What You Hear. Be mindful of what you allow into your mind and emotions. If a conversation, show, post, or song feeds fear, compromise, or comparison, step back or turn it off. Whisper, "I choose to be good ground."

Evening: Turn the Soil Again. Read Romans 10:17 aloud. Revisit your circled area. Ask, "Lord, what did You show me about my heart today?" Write a short reflection and a sentence of gratitude.

By week's end, you will begin to notice increased tenderness, quicker conviction, and renewed desire to protect what God plants. These are the early signs of fallow ground being broken up and a heart becoming good soil.

Closing Prayer

"Father, thank You for showing me the soil of my heart. Where I have become hard, break me gently. Where I have been shallow, deepen my roots. Where thorns have crowded Your Word, pull them up by the root. Teach me to guard what You plant and to water it through meditation. Renew my mind until it mirrors the mind of Christ. Let the early fruit of Your Spirit grow in me, and prepare me for the greater harvest still to come. In Jesus' name, Amen."

Chapter 3

The Gardener and the Living Seeds

"Now the parable is this: The seed is the word of God."
(Luke 8:11, KJV)

The rain had stopped just before dawn, leaving the world washed and breathless. A low mist clung to the garden rows, drifting like pale threads across the wooden fence. Elias wiped the fog from his window and stared out at the soil he had spent weeks preparing. Every furrow was straight; every row measured with care. The ground looked ready, almost eager, like a canvas stretched tight and waiting for its first stroke of color.

Still, something was missing.

Elias remained at the window longer than he intended. He watched the mist thin and reform, thinning again as though the morning itself could not decide whether to reveal the land or conceal it. His hands rested on the sill, roughened by years of labor, yet trembling slightly now. Preparation had always been his comfort. Measuring. Planning. Tending. Those were actions he understood. Waiting without instruction unsettled him.

He had prepared the soil as his father taught him; slowly, deliberately, refusing to rush what demanded patience. Each furrow had been cut with care, each stone removed, each clod broken down until the earth lay loose and receptive. There were no shortcuts in this kind of work. The ground bore witness to that truth.

And yet, despite all of it, the sense lingered: preparation alone was not enough.

He inhaled deeply, the scent of damp earth filling his lungs. It smelled like promise, but also like risk. Once planted, seeds could not be retrieved unchanged. Whatever went into the soil would emerge transformed, or not at all.

He turned to the workbench. A small linen pouch sat in the center, sealed with red wax. The handwritten label, dark and deliberate, read: "Eternal Life."

The name unsettled him.

Elias had seen many labels in his life; names of herbs, grains, flowers destined for kitchens or markets, but this one resisted easy classification. Eternal Life was not something one planted in rows or harvested by season. It did not belong to calendars or ledgers. And yet here it was, written plainly, without ornament or explanation, as if the sender assumed Elias would understand.

He searched his memory for when he first learned the phrase. It surfaced slowly: childhood evenings by lamplight, his father reading aloud, voice steady and reverent. Words about life that could not be stolen by moth or rust. About something given freely, yet never cheaply.

Elias had believed those words then, without effort. Belief came easily to a child. Now belief demanded something more deliberate. Something costly.

Elias traced the letters slowly. The package had arrived the day before, delivered by a quiet traveler who did not explain, only the cryptic instruction: "These are not like other seeds. Handle them with faith."

Now Elias broke the seal. Inside were twelve small kernels. Ordinary at first glance. Brown, dull, unimpressive. He turned them over in his palm, half expecting a spark or a glow, but there was nothing.

The seeds felt cool against his skin, lighter than he expected. He weighed them one by one, noting their sameness. No marking distinguished one from another. If scattered among common grain, no one would notice their absence.

He wondered briefly whether this was a test.

Faith often was.

The temptation to doubt rose quietly, without accusation. How many times had he trusted what looked ordinary, only to be disappointed? How many seasons had ended in loss despite careful obedience? The questions did not shout; they whispered. That made them more dangerous.

Elias closed his hand around the seeds and exhaled slowly. "If the power were obvious," he murmured, "there would be no need for trust."

He let out a soft sigh. "They look no different than what I have planted before."

Yet something in him stirred. A memory surfaced, faint but firm, like a voice rising from the depths.

"The power is never in the shell, my son. It is in what you cannot see."

His father's words, spoken long ago.

His father's voice lingered with unusual clarity. Elias could almost see him now; stooped slightly with age, hands stained dark with soil, eyes constantly scanning beyond what was immediately visible. He had spoken often of seeds, but never merely as objects. Seeds were lessons; promises wrapped in restraint.

"Anyone can admire the harvest," his father once said. "Few honor the burial."

At the time, Elias had nodded politely, not fully grasping the weight of those words. Burial sounded like a loss. Like surrender. Now he understood: burial was an act of hope, not despair. You buried only what you believed would rise.

Elias stepped outside and walked to the first row. The soil welcomed his hand as he pressed the first seed beneath the surface. He covered it with gentle precision, then another, and another, until all twelve were buried like small secrets entrusted to the earth.

The day passed quietly.

Quiet did not mean empty.

Elias moved through his usual tasks, yet each motion felt slower, more attentive. He noticed the sound of his footsteps against the packed earth, the creak of the fence in the light breeze, the way the sun traced its steady arc overhead. Everything continued as it always had, and yet nothing felt the same.

He resisted the urge to recheck the rows. Seeds did not respond to scrutiny. They responded to trust.

Instead, he occupied his hands elsewhere, repairing a loose hinge, sharpening tools already sharp enough. Still, his thoughts returned again and again to the soil, not with anxiety, but with expectation restrained by discipline.

Faith, he was learning, required restraint.

By evening, the mist had lifted, and the moon rose full and bright, pouring silver over the field. Elias walked the rows one last time. As he neared the center, he stopped. Something beneath the soil seemed to flicker.

He knelt quickly, heart pounding. The ground pulsed with a faint glow, dim but rhythmic, like the heartbeat of an ember under ash.

He reached out, but before his fingers touched the soil, the light vanished.

Elias stayed there on his knees, breath visible in the cool night air. Awe wrapped around him, still and heavy. He whispered, "The Word is alive. It breathes."

The words surprised him as they left his mouth. He had not planned to speak to them. They emerged as a confession more than a declaration.

Alive.

Breathing.

He pressed his palm against the earth, feeling its warmth seep into his skin. The sensation comforted him. Life was at work whether he observed it or not. Growth did not require witnesses. It required time.

Rising to his feet, Elias felt lighter, though the mystery remained unresolved. Perhaps that was the point. Faith was not certainty; it was allegiance in the absence of sight.

Morning brought no visible sprouts, yet the soil felt warm beneath his fingertips. Birds gathered along the fence as if drawn by a sound too soft for human ears, hopping and chirping with unusual alertness.

Their presence unsettled him, not with fear but with wonder. Animals often sensed what humans overlooked. Creation itself seemed attentive, alert to something unfolding beneath the surface.

Elias recalled a verse his father once quoted: about all of creation groaning and waiting. Waiting; for what? Redemption, perhaps. Or simply the fulfillment of what had already been promised.

He watched the birds scatter suddenly, lifting as one, startled by nothing he could see. The fence stood empty again, the field quiet, but his sense of anticipation deepened.

Elias stood, lifting his eyes toward heaven. "Your Word lives," he said quietly. "And I will keep it buried until it breaks open."

Later that day, Hannah found him at the window again, staring at the rows with a look she had not seen in years. She placed a hand on his arm.

"You are waiting for something," she said.

"Yes," Elias replied. "And I think heaven is waiting with me."

She smiled, understanding more than she said. "Then let us tend the waiting."

Hannah had always understood waiting differently than he did. Where Elias measured time in seasons and yields, she measured it in faithfulness. In her presence, waiting did not feel passive. It felt purposeful.

Together they prepared the evening meal in near silence, each motion unhurried. When she read aloud later, her voice carried a steadiness that anchored him. Scripture did not rush to conclusions. It unfolded patiently, inviting the listener to dwell rather than hurry ahead.

That evening, she read aloud from Luke.

"Now the parable is this: The seed is the word of God."

The words resonated through the room like truth striking a bell. Elias felt it deep in his chest. The seeds were not ordinary. They represented something living, something divine, something planted not just in soil but in him.

When night fell again, Elias stood by the window once more. The field lay still, but not silent. The silence felt full, as though roots were moving beneath the surface, finding their paths, breaking the darkness in secret.

Life was beginning where no eye could see.

As the days followed, nothing dramatic occurred. No sudden shoots broke the surface. No blaze of light returned. Yet Elias felt no disappointment. Something had shifted within him. He had entrusted something precious to the soil and, in doing so, entrusted himself as well.

Faith was not the absence of doubt. It was the decision to remain faithful even when doubt lingered.

And Elias knew he was witnessing more than a garden. He was watching faith take root.

Eternal
Life

The Living Seed

"Now the parable is this: The seed is the word of God."
(Luke 8:11, KJV)

"For the word of God is quick, and powerful, and sharper than any twoedged sword, piercing even to the dividing asunder of soul and spirit, and of the joints and marrow, and is a discerner of the thoughts and intents of the heart."
(Hebrews 4:12, KJV)

Every seed carries a hidden world inside it. A single kernel, unimpressive in the hand, contains the blueprint of a tree that can outlast a generation. You do not command a seed to grow. You simply place it in the right environment, and its embedded life does the rest.

The Word of God works the same way.

Elias saw it with his own eyes. The seeds he planted seemed ordinary until they were planted in the soil. But once buried, they pulsed with a quiet light, alive beneath the surface. Nothing changed above ground at first, no sprout, no sign, no confirmation. Yet in the unseen places, life was moving.

God's Word behaves this way in the believer. It works underground, long before it breaks through the surface of behavior or emotion. You may not feel anything the moment you read Scripture. You may not understand how God is shaping you. But the Word is active the moment it enters surrendered soil.

Jesus explained the mystery: "The seed is the word of God."

A seed is not a symbol. It is living potential. The Word is not only information. It is living power.

That is why Hebrews says it is "quick," meaning alive. It searches, separates, cuts, heals, exposes, and builds. No human book can do that. Only the Word of God carries the breath of God.

The Word Works Beneath the Surface

"The wind bloweth where it listeth, ... so is every one that is born of the Spirit."
(John 3:8, KJV)

You cannot always explain how the Spirit works in you, but you can learn to recognize His movement. Elias did not understand the glowing seeds, but he trusted the Giver. Their life was visible, even when the growth was not.

Likewise, when the Word enters your heart, the Spirit begins rearranging things you didn't know needed moving. Convictions sharpen. Old desires lose their strength. Hunger for God increases. The Word begins dividing soul from spirit, exposing thoughts, cleansing motives, renewing patterns.

You do not force this growth. You cooperate with it.

The heart that welcomes the Word is like soil warming in the morning sun. Faith softens it. Surrender opens it. Meditation keeps it moist. And slowly, the seed awakens.

The DNA of Scripture

Every living seed reproduces according to its kind. Apple seeds cannot become an Olive tree. Wheat seeds cannot yield weeds.

So it is with the Word.

The Word of peace produces peace. The Word of righteousness produces obedience. The Word of promise produces hope. The

Word of truth creates freedom.

This is divine order:

The Word can only bear the nature of the One who spoke it. When Scripture enters good soil, it carries the nature of Christ into the believer. That is why spiritual growth is never self-manufactured. You cannot produce Christlike fruit through effort alone. Christ grows Christ within you through His Word.

Elias did not need to manipulate the seeds to glow. Their life was already inside them. He placed them where life could express itself.

You must do the same with Scripture.

Handle it reverently. Speak it aloud. Meditate on it. Guard it in your heart.

The Word does not need your brilliance to grow. It requires your agreement.

Receiving the Seed by Faith

"And he said, So is the kingdom of God, as if a man should cast seed into the ground; … and the seed should spring and grow up, he knoweth not how."
(Mark 4:26-27, KJV)

Faith activates the Word. Not intellect. Not emotion. Not curiosity. Faith.

Faith is the warmth that calls the seed to life. Faith is the atmosphere in which the Spirit moves. Faith is the "yes" that opens the soil.

You don't need theological expertise to grow spiritually; you need willingness. When you believe what God says enough to plant it in the soil of your heart, the Word begins its invisible work.

Faith is not passive. Faith plants. Faith waters. Faith protects. Faith waits.

Elias did not dig up the seed to check its progress. He trusted what had been spoken to him: "Handle them with faith." Growth belongs to God. Waiting belongs to us.

Recognizing When the Word is Growing in You

Spiritual growth rarely begins with fireworks. It starts like Elias's glowing field, subtle, quiet, almost imperceptible.

You will know the seed is sprouting when:

You respond differently to familiar temptations. You find unexpected peace in stressful moments. You hunger for Scripture instead of forcing yourself to read it. You sense conviction quickly and welcome correction. You speak more truth than opinion, more blessing than complaint.

These are the first tender shoots breaking the surface.

They are small, but they are alive.

Peter described this hunger as a sign of growth:

"As newborn babes, desire the sincere milk of the word, that ye may grow thereby:"
(1 Peter 2:2, KJV)

Growth begins with desire. Desire begins with the Spirit. The Spirit starts with the seed. The more you welcome the Word, the more the Word reshapes you. What God plants in secret eventually appears in strength. So keep planting. Keep listening. Keep meditating. Keep watering the soil with faith.

The seed you carry today contains the fruit you will walk in tomorrow.

Reflection & Practice

1. Reflection
The seed of the Word is always alive, but it only grows where the soil cooperates. Ask yourself slowly: Have I been treating Scripture as information to read, or as a living seed to receive, plant, and protect? Where have I expected fruit without first tending the unseen soil where the seed must take root? Invite the Holy Spirit to show you specific areas, not just general ideas. Let Him answer honestly, and resist the urge to explain, defend, or hurry past what He reveals.

2. Scripture Meditation
Read this passage aloud, slowly, as if you are handling something living:

"For the word of God is quick, and powerful, and sharper than any twoedged sword, piercing even to the dividing asunder of soul and spirit, and of the joints and marrow, and is a discerner of the thoughts and intents of the heart."
(Hebrews 4:12, KJV)

Then read this second verse:

"And he said, So is the kingdom of God, as if a man should cast seed into the ground; And should sleep, and rise night and day, and the seed should spring and grow up, he knoweth not how."
(Mark 4:26-27, KJV)

Let these truths settle in your heart: The Word is alive, though growth is often hidden. It is the Spirit that does the work. Your part is to plant and to protect.

3. Prayer of Alignment

Holy Spirit, I bring You the soil of my heart. Where Your Word has stayed on the surface, plant it deeper. Where distraction has stolen the seed, restore what has been taken. Where stones of pride, fear, or disappointment block the roots, uncover them and carry them away. Where thorns crowd out Your voice, uproot them completely. Make my heart good ground that welcomes Your Word with reverence and expectation. Awaken my hunger again. Let the seed You have planted live, breathe, and reshape me from the inside out. I yield the soil to You. You give the growth. In Jesus' name, amen.

4. Action Step

Plant one verse intentionally this week. Not three, not ten, one.

Choose a verse that stands out from this chapter's teaching, for example: Luke 8:11, Hebrews 4:12, 1 Peter 2:2, John 6:63.

Write it on a card or in your journal.

Each day, do three simple things with it:

Read it aloud.

Picture it. Let your imagination form a scene or image.

Personalize it. Please put it in the first person.

Example: "The seed is the word of God" becomes: "The seed God plants in me is His Word, and it is alive in me."

Let this single verse become a seed you plant on purpose, not a sentence you skim.

5. Practice for the Week
Keep a simple daily rhythm around your chosen verse.

Morning: Warm the Soil. Speak your verse aloud before you begin the day. Place your hand over your heart and pray, "Lord, let this seed take root in me today."

Midday: Water the Seed. Pause for sixty seconds. Whisper the verse again. Ask, "Holy Spirit, what are You growing in me through this Word right now?"

Evening: Notice the Sprouts. Read Mark 4:26 to 27 once more. Write one line in your journal beginning with, "Today I saw the seed growing when I…"Even if the change seems small, record it. What you record, you reinforce.

By the end of the week, watch for increased awareness, tenderness, or quiet conviction. These are the first shoots breaking the surface, proof that the Word is working in you and that the Spirit is faithfully cultivating the life of Christ within your heart.

Closing Prayer

"Father, thank You for the gift of Your Word, living, breathing, and eternal. Teach me to handle it not as ink on a page but as a seed carrying Your very life. Prepare my heart to receive, to guard, and to grow what You plant. Where I have read without faith, awaken my expectancy. Where I have spoken without belief, renew my confession. Let the light of Your Spirit hover over every verse I read, and cause what You've sown to spring forth in due time.

Make my life a garden that bears Your image, filled with the fruit of Your Spirit, rooted in love, watered by grace, and open to Your rain of righteousness. In Jesus' name, Amen."

Chapter 4

Hidden Growth

"And he said, So is the kingdom of God, as if a man should cast seed into the ground; And should sleep, and rise night and day, and the seed should spring and grow up, he knoweth not how."
(Mark 4:26-27, KJV)

The morning opened with the scent of firewood and fresh bread drifting through the small farmhouse. Elias sat on the porch, hands wrapped around a warm clay cup, watching thin threads of steam rise and mingle with his breath in the cool air. From inside, Hannah hummed a psalm as she worked near the hearth. Her soft singing had become part of their mornings, a reminder that gratitude must come before labor.

Elias listened to Hannah's voice rise and fall, familiar and steady. It did not rush the words or embellish them. She sang as one who believed the meaning mattered more than the melody. Over the years, her quiet devotion had shaped the rhythm of their home. Prayer was not something they added to the day. It was something the day grew from.

He lifted the cup to his lips and let the warmth settle him. Mornings like this carried a gentle weight, the kind that asked nothing urgent but invited attentiveness. The stillness did not feel empty. It felt expectant, as though the day itself waited for permission to unfold.

Beyond the porch, the small field lay still. The rows of soil were dark and quiet, their surfaces unbroken. Weeks had passed since Elias planted the twelve mysterious seeds, yet not a single green sprout had appeared. Still, he had risen every dawn to bless the ground, trusting the unseen work beneath it.

Others in the village had begun to notice his routine. Some nodded politely as he passed. Others offered quiet glances filled with curiosity or concern. A few had asked questions he did not know how to answer. Elias did not resent them. He understood the discomfort of waiting without evidence. He had lived there himself.

Each morning, blessing the ground had become an act of surrender. He did not speak loudly or dramatically. He simply acknowledged what he believed to be true, even when his senses argued otherwise. Faith, he was learning, was sustained by repetition. Not repetition born of fear, but of trust.

He closed his eyes and whispered, "Father, You said the Word is alive. I trust that You are working where I cannot see."

The quiet carried his prayer like incense. A verse lingered in his heart, one Hannah had read to him the night before.

"For we walk by faith, not by sight."

Elias had heard the verse countless times, yet it met him differently now. Once, it had sounded like instruction. Now it felt like an invitation. Walking by faith was not blind. It was choosing to let truth guide him when sight fell short.

He exhaled slowly, allowing the words to settle. The field beyond the porch remained unchanged, but his heart felt steadier. There was a quiet strength in anchoring himself to something eternal while standing in the ordinary.

Footsteps approached behind him. A small voice broke the silence.

"Father, are you going to the field again?"

Elias turned to find Micah standing in the doorway, still fighting sleep, his hair disheveled and his eyes half closed with drowsiness. Elias reached for his hand.

"Yes, come with me."

Micah's hand felt small in his own, warm and trusting. Elias noticed how naturally the boy followed, without hesitation or questions. Children understood trust before they learned to doubt. Elias wondered when that shift happened, when believing required explanation.

They walked barefoot through the dew-covered grass. Birds flitted between the fence posts, filling the air with bright chatter as though they carried their own morning liturgy. Elias slowed his pace, allowing Micah to remain beside him rather than trailing behind. Teaching, he had learned, happened best when shared steps matched.

Micah followed close behind his father, stepping into his footprints as they entered the rows. The sight stirred something deep within Elias. He remembered doing the same as a child, aligning his steps with his father's, trusting that the path was safe because it had already been walked. The memory carried both comfort and responsibility. He was no longer the one learning where to place his feet. He was the one leaving marks behind.

When they reached the center of the field, Elias knelt. Micah watched him, puzzled.

"Father," he said, "why do you keep looking at dirt? Every day you come here, and every day it looks the same."

Elias brushed his fingers across the soil's surface. "Because even when nothing appears to be happening, the work has already begun beneath the surface."

Micah crouched beside him, running his hand through the loose dirt. "But how do you know something is growing? Nothing has happened."

Elias studied his son's face, recognizing the question beneath the question. It was not really about the soil. It was about disappointment. About the quiet ache of expectation unmet.

He placed a steady hand on the boy's shoulder. "Faith does not begin with seeing, Micah. It begins with believing. Do you remember the Scripture?" He spoke it gently. "Now faith is the substance of things hoped for, the evidence of things not seen."

Micah frowned, trying to make sense of it. "So we just wait?"

"Yes," Elias answered. "We wait, and we keep the soil soft with trust. A seed strengthens its roots before it ever shows its face. It grows down before it grows up."

The phrase lingered between them. Elias had spoken it often to himself in recent weeks. Growth unseen was not wasted growth. Strength hidden was not absence. The deepest work usually happened where no one applauded.

Micah stared at the ground as if hoping something would break through that very moment. When nothing did, he sighed.

"But it feels like nothing is happening."

Elias nodded. "I know. I've felt that too. But the ground doesn't stay quiet because it's empty. It stays quiet because something is taking hold underneath."

He paused, letting the silence speak for him. Some truths settle better when left untouched. The earth before them remained undisturbed, but Elias felt peace rising gently within his chest, and waiting no longer felt like a delay. It felt like a partnership with something larger than himself.

They stood together in the quiet. The morning wind brushed against their faces, calm and gentle. Elias remembered the Shepherd's voice from his dream, the voice that had marked him and would not let him go. It echoed again in his heart now, soft but unmistakable.

"I will be with you in the field and in the furrow, in the word and in the work."

He whispered the truth beneath his breath. "Alive even when unseen."

The words felt like an anchor. Elias held them quietly, committing them to memory. He sensed that this truth would need to be recalled often in the days ahead, not only for himself but also for Micah.

As they turned to head back home, the edge of the sun crested the horizon. Light poured over the furrows like gold, warming the earth. Elias paused, a swell of assurance rising in him. The words of Jesus came to mind, steady and comforting.

"The seed should spring and grow up, he knoweth not how."

The mystery of it no longer troubled him. There was relief in not needing to understand every mechanism. Trust did not require explanation; only faithfulness was required.

Micah tugged his father's hand. "What does that mean?"

Elias looked down at his son and smiled. "It means the seed knows what to do. Our part is to trust the One who made it."

Micah nodded slowly, absorbing more than he understood. They walked back toward the farmhouse, the smell of warm bread meeting them halfway.

That night, after the household had settled into the softness of evening, Elias knelt beside his bed.

"Lord," he prayed, "teach me to wait well, and help my son learn the peace that comes from trusting You."

Elias remained kneeling long after the prayer ended. He felt no urgency to rise. The room was quiet, the kind of quiet that felt inhabited rather than empty. He sensed the same unseen work occurring within himself that he trusted beneath the soil.

Outside, deep beneath the earth, the seed split open in the hidden dark. A root pushed downward, steady and determined, reaching for deeper strength before it ever approached the surface.

The seed was working.

The waiting had not been empty.

Faith Beneath the Surface

"And he said, So is the kingdom of God, as if a man should cast seed into the ground; And should sleep, and rise night and day, and the seed should spring and grow up, he knoweth not how."
(Mark 4:26-27, KJV)

Every seed carries a mystery inside it. Its entire future is hidden within the shell, yet nothing of that future can be seen when it is buried. The breaking happens in silence. The roots reach downward long before any stem reaches upward. The seed does not resist the darkness. It yields to the design written within it.

Faith grows the same way. Its real work begins where sight ends. Sight demands evidence before belief, but faith believes long before evidence appears. Faith and sight move in opposite directions.

"Now faith is the substance of things hoped for, the evidence of things not seen."
(Hebrews 11:1, KJV)

God does His deepest work in places the eyes cannot measure, and the hands cannot manipulate. What was happening beneath the soil of Elias's vineyard illustrates this perfectly. While nothing appeared to have changed above ground, the seed was unfolding in hidden places. It was pushing, breaking, breathing, and stretching. Life was working where no one could see it.

Your faith does the same. Most of what God forms in you is formed beneath the surface.

You cannot force a sprout into existence. You can only keep the soil soft, keep your heart receptive, and keep your posture surrendered. Faith does not accelerate growth. Faith protects growth. It guards the ground while the Word accomplishes its work.

"So then faith cometh by hearing, and hearing by the word of God."
(Romans 10:17, KJV)

Notice that the Scripture does not say faith comes by having heard once. It says hearing, a continual posture. Faith grows by repetition. Each time you hear the Word spoken through Scripture, through preaching, or through your own voice declaring His promises, you are tilling the soil of your heart again.

This is why your words matter. Your heart is always listening to your mouth.

"Death and life are in the power of the tongue: ..."
(Proverbs 18:21, KJV)

Truth strengthens the soil because speaking God's Word over your own life anchors His promises in your heart. Complaint weakens the soil by rehearsing what is wrong until it hardens into belief. Faith waters the seed as words of trust create space for growth. Doubt scorches the soil when fear-filled speech dries out what God is trying to cultivate.

If what you say in the waiting season contradicts what God has spoken, then your words are working against your own prayer.

When God sows His Word in you, He asks for cooperation, not control. You are not the creator of growth. You are the caretaker of the environment. Meditation, gratitude, and stillness are ways of caring for what He planted. Every time you repeat His promise aloud, you water what is unseen. Every time you thank Him before results appear, you warm the soil of trust.

Faith beneath the surface is not loud, but it is alive. It does not demand to see the harvest. It rests in the certainty that the Word will accomplish what God intends.

"So shall my word be that goeth forth out of my mouth: It shall not return unto me void, But it shall accomplish that which I please, And it shall prosper in the thing whereto I sent it."
(Isaiah 55:11, KJV)

This is the miracle and the mystery of faith beneath the surface.

The Discipline of Waiting

"...Behold, the husbandman waiteth for the precious fruit of the earth, and hath long patience for it, until he receive the early and latter rain."
(James 5:7, KJV)

Waiting is not a delay in God's plan; it is part of the plan. The farmer who plants does not interrogate the ground each morning but trusts the design within the seed. In the same way, you and I are invited to trust the design of the Word God has planted in us. Waiting is not inactivity; it is the quiet strength of faith, choosing to remain present before God while He works beneath the surface.

You cannot rush what God has ordained to ripen in time. Each stage of spiritual growth unfolds in His timing, from rooting and stretching through strengthening and fruiting.

"Rest in the Lord, and wait patiently for him: ..."
(Psalm 37:7, KJV)

To rest is not to do nothing. It is to surrender your will to His. Rest is faith refusing to push ahead of God. It is the posture that says, "Your pace is better than my pressure." In that surrender, the soul learns to trust God's timing more than its own urgency. And as trust deepens, striving loosens its grip, making room for God's peace to steady every step.

Faith begins the work. Patience sustains it.

> *"That ye be not slothful, but followers of them who through faith and patience inherit the promises."*
> (Hebrews 6:12, KJV)

Without patience, faith collapses at the first delay. But when patience joins hands with faith, the unseen work of God continues without interruption.

Faithful waiting also purifies your speech. Waiting without faith produces complaint. Waiting with faith produces praise. When you speak gratitude in a silent season, you align yourself with God's rhythm. Gratitude is the sunlight of the spirit. It keeps the soil warm when nothing appears to be sprouting.

Jesus said the seed grows while the man "knoweth not how." The mystery of faith is not understanding the how, but trusting the Who. Every promise has its appointed season, and every season requires endurance. Roots must grow deep before branches can bear the weight of fruit.

Waiting is God's way of strengthening you before He multiplies you.

What Hidden Growth Teaches

Hidden growth is never wasted. God uses seasons of unseen growth to teach you what seasons of visible fruitfulness cannot.

Hidden growth teaches trust, because you must believe before you see. Hidden growth teaches humility, because you cannot take credit for what only God can do. Hidden growth teaches stewardship, because your job is not to manufacture life but to protect its environment. Hidden growth teaches discernment, because you learn to distinguish God's whisper from your own.

You may not feel progress while God works beneath the surface. But every quiet hour of faithfulness becomes visible fruit in due time.

> *"(For we walk by faith, not by sight:)"*
> (2 Corinthians 5:7, KJV)

Faith beneath the surface is God's way of forming strength that cannot be shaken, even when storms arrive in later chapters of life.

Reflection & Practice

1. Reflection

Waiting seasons reveal what we genuinely believe beneath the surface. Ask yourself slowly: When God seems silent, do I tend the soil of my heart with faith, or do impatience, doubt, and complaint begin to harden it? What does my inner response to waiting reveal about the condition of my soil? Sit with these questions honestly. Let the Holy Spirit bring clarity without defensiveness or hurry.

Allow Him to show you the places where waiting has weakened your trust and the places where waiting has strengthened it.

2. Scripture Meditation

Read these verses aloud with attention, allowing their truth to settle like water sinking into soil:

> *"And he said, So is the kingdom of God, as if a man should cast seed into the ground; And should sleep, and rise night and day, and the seed should spring and grow up, he knoweth not how."*
> (Mark 4:26-27, KJV)

"Rest in the Lord, and wait patiently for him: ..."
(Psalm 37:7, KJV)

"So shall my word be that goeth forth out of my mouth: It shall not return unto me void, But it shall accomplish that which I please, ..."
(Isaiah 55:11, KJV)

Hold this truth gently: God's Word is working even when nothing seems to be happening.

3. Prayer of Alignment

Father, teach me to trust You in the unseen places. Quiet the restless thoughts that rise in waiting. Break the habit of rushing ahead of Your timing. Fill my waiting with worship instead of worry. Let my words agree with what You have spoken, not with what my fears whisper.

Holy Spirit, soften the soil of my heart. Keep me patient, grateful, and surrendered while the seed grows beneath the surface. Help me trust what You are doing in secret long before I see fruit in the light. I choose Your timing, Your pace, and Your process. In Jesus' name, amen.

4. Action Step

Practice one intentional act of gratitude every time impatience rises this week. Whenever you feel frustrated, delayed, or anxious about something you are waiting on:

Stop for five seconds.

Take one slow breath.

Speak a sentence of gratitude tied to God's faithfulness.

Examples: "Lord, thank You that Your Word is working right now." "Thank You that Your timing is wiser than mine." "Thank You that roots are forming where I cannot see yet."

Gratitude warms the soil. It creates the environment where the seed can grow.

5. Practice for the Week

Build a simple rhythm that keeps your heart soft while God works in the unseen.

Morning: Water the Seed. Read Mark 4:26-27 aloud. Pray, "Lord, grow what You planted in me today."

Midday: Guard Your Words. Pause for thirty seconds and notice your inner dialogue. If you hear a complaint or doubt, replace it with Scripture. Say, "Faith comes by hearing, and I choose to hear Your Word today."

Evening: Record hidden growth. Write one observation of quiet change: a calmer reaction, gentler patience, or renewed confidence.

End of Week: Reaffirm His Process. Read James 5:7-8. Declare, "Lord, I trust Your process, and I welcome Your timing."

This rhythm trains your heart to see what waiting often hides: God is working, even now.

Closing Prayer

"Father, You are Lord over seasons of hidden growth. Teach me to trust You when nothing appears to change. Help me to rest in Your pace, not my own. Guard my words so they speak faith instead of fear. Let gratitude rise where complaint once lived, and let patience take root deep within my heart. May each unseen day strengthen me in ways I cannot yet measure, until Your promise bears fruit in Your perfect time. In Jesus' name, Amen.

PART II

Speaking in Faith: Releasing What God Has Conceived

The hidden work of faith always begins in silence. Beneath the soil of your heart, the Word has been planted, pressed, and watered. What was once unseen is now ready to emerge.

Every seed follows a divine order: Spirit → Heart → Soul → Body. The Spirit receives the Word from God. The Heart believes and guards it. The Soul (your thoughts and emotions) aligns with it. And the Body acts it out in obedience.

This divine order is the holy progression of transformation: from invisible truth to visible fruit. The same Spirit who whispered to you in stillness will now teach you how to speak what He has conceived. For creation itself began this way:

> *"...And the Spirit of God moved upon the face of the waters. And God said, Let there be light:"*
> (Genesis 1:2-3, KJV)

God's speaking was never separate from His doing. The Spirit was already in motion, poised to carry out His will the instant His Word was released. When God spoke, the Spirit enacted what the

Word commanded. There was no delay, because in God, Word and Spirit move as one.

As Scripture declares:

"By the word of the Lord were the heavens made; And all the host of them by the breath of his mouth."
(Psalm 33:6, KJV)

What was conceived in His Spirit became manifest through His Word. That same divine pattern now operates in you.

When the Word of God is planted in your heart, it is not meant to remain buried; it must rise to your lips before it can shape your world. Your confession is the bridge between faith's conception and faith's completion.

You have learned how to prepare the ground. Now you will learn how to release the life within the seed.

Chapter 5

God Spoke Before He Saw

"And God said, Let there be light: and there was light."
(Genesis 1:3, KJV)

Morning light filtered through the workshop windows in soft bands, catching dust motes that drifted like tiny sparks in the air. The smell of fresh wood filled the room, warm and sweet. Elias stood at the large carving table, a block of olive wood secured beneath his hands. The curves of the grain shimmered faintly as if waiting to be awakened.

The workshop had always been a place of quiet formation. Tools hung neatly along the walls, each one worn smooth by years of faithful use. Every surface bore the marks of patience rather than haste. Elias had learned long ago that what endured was rarely rushed. Wood resisted force but yielded to understanding.

Micah entered quietly, wiping sleep from his eyes. At thirteen, he had grown taller, yet there was still a boyish wonder in the way he watched his father work. He lingered near the doorway for a moment, absorbing the stillness, the way one might pause before stepping onto holy ground.

Elias glanced up and smiled, recognizing the look. He handed Micah a smaller carving tool, its handle fitted to the boy's grip. "Come," he said, "today you will learn something more than craft."

Micah took the tool, feeling its weight, studying the unshaped block before him. "What are we making?"

Elias did not answer immediately. He brushed his fingers along the wood's surface. "Before you answer that, tell me what you see."

Micah turned the block slowly in his hands. He examined the grain, the knots, the imperfections. "I see a block," he said finally. "I do not see anything else yet."

"That is because you are looking with your eyes only," Elias replied gently. "A craftsman must learn to see with his spirit first."

Micah frowned, unsure. "How can I see something that is not there?"

Elias lifted his own chisel and held it loosely, not as a weapon but as an extension of his will. "That is how God created the world. He spoke before He saw. The vision was already alive in Him, even when nothing yet existed."

He guided Micah to stand beside him. "Watch."

Elias touched the tip of the chisel to the wood, steady and deliberate. "Inside this grain, a shape already lives. My voice declares what my hands will reveal."

With a controlled movement, he carved the first line. Wood curled away in soft ribbons, falling quietly to the floor. "This is how God worked in Genesis. He saw light in His spirit, then He spoke, 'Let there be light,' and the light obeyed His voice."

Micah stared, breath held, as the line deepened. "So the statue is already in there," he said slowly. "You are just uncovering it."

"Exactly," Elias said. "And the same is true with the promises God gives you. They begin as vision, as something unseen but certain. When you speak what God has conceived in your heart, you agree with His intention."

Micah lowered his gaze to his own block of wood. He hesitated. "But, Father, what if I speak something and nothing happens?"

Elias set down his tools and leaned closer, lowering his voice. "Then you must learn the same patience God used in creation. A seed does not sprout the day it is planted, but the moment it is buried in the soil, something has already begun beneath the surface. In the same way, God's Word starts its work the moment it is spoken, before your eyes can see the result."

Micah nodded slowly, absorbing the weight of the idea. "So God speaks what He intends to reveal."

"Yes," Elias said, placing his hand over Micah's. "And those made in His image do the same. Our words shape what our hands will one day hold."

He guided Micah's tool to the surface of the wood. Together, they carved a gentle curve. Micah's hands trembled slightly, but the line held. Elias did not correct him. He let the moment teach.

A look of amazement came over Micah's face. "I can see the shape now," he said quietly. "Just a little, but it is there."

Elias smiled. "That is how revelation works. God shows you pieces. When you declare them, they begin to take form."

They worked side by side for the next hour, the workshop settling into a steady rhythm. The sound of carving filled the space, soft and measured. Shavings gathered around their feet like fallen leaves. Micah's movements grew surer as confidence replaced hesitation. He began to anticipate the grain rather than resist it.

From time to time, Elias paused, not to instruct, but to observe. Teaching did not always require words. Sometimes, presence was enough.

When they finally stepped back, a faint outline of a lamb had begun to appear in Micah's block. The figure was still rough, its edges unfinished, but unmistakably alive.

Micah gasped. "I did not know this was inside."

Elias rested a hand on his son's shoulder. "Heaven always places more in you than you see at first. When God speaks to your spirit, He reveals what is possible. Your words then align with His, and your life begins to take shape."

Micah studied the small lamb, running his fingers along the emerging form. "So the more I say what God says, the clearer things become."

"Yes," Elias replied softly. "Do not wait to see before you speak. Speak because you believe."

They stood together in quiet satisfaction as the morning sun deepened across the workshop floor, illuminating both the finished and the unfinished alike.

Outside, the vineyard rustled in a gentle wind, as if creation itself agreed.

Speaking What God Conceived

"And God said, Let there be light: and there was light."
(Genesis 1:3, KJV)

"Through faith we understand that the worlds were framed by the word of God, so that things which are seen were not made of things which do appear."
(Hebrews 11:3, KJV)

"By the word of the Lord were the heavens made; And all the host of them by the breath of his mouth."
(Psalm 33:6, KJV)

Creation began with a voice.

Before God ever formed a mountain, shaped a valley, or set the stars in place, He spoke. The universe did not emerge by accident or chaos; it was created by deliberate command. Light existed first by God's will, then by His Word, and finally in the world He brought into being.

This is Heaven's order: Conception in the Spirit, declaration through the Word, manifestation by the Spirit's power. God imagines, God speaks, and God brings forth.

And because we were made in His image, this order is the blueprint of how faith operates in us.

Made in His Likeness

"And God said, Let us make man in our image, after our likeness:"
(Genesis 1:26, KJV)

God did not merely give you a voice. He gave you a voice patterned after His own.

Humans are the only part of creation designed to collaborate with God through speech. Animals communicate instinctively. Angels carry out God's commands. But humanity alone was entrusted to speak in agreement with God, exercising authority within the world He made.

Your voice is not just a tool for communication. It is an instrument of alignment. It is a vessel through which Heaven touches earth.

God formed the worlds through His Word, and you frame your life through yours. Not because your voice is divine, but because your voice was created to echo the divine.

The Word Spoken Through You

Heaven responds to Scripture spoken in faith.

"Bless the Lord, ye his angels, That excel in strength, that do his commandments, Hearkening unto the voice of his word."
(Psalm 103:20, KJV)

The angels do not obey your opinion. They obey God's Word voiced through you.

This is why the enemy works harder to silence your confession than your thoughts. Thoughts privately held cannot confront darkness. Words spoken in faith pierce the atmosphere and command movement.

When you declare Scripture aloud, you are not trying to persuade God. You are agreeing with what He has already decreed, giving earthly expression to Heaven's will and releasing the authority of His Word into your circumstances. Heaven recognizes its own language.

When God's Word leaves your mouth, the Spirit and the angels respond as if God Himself had spoken, not because you are God, but because you are His vessel.

The Connection Between Seeing and Speaking

Before Elias spoke a blessing over his children and vineyard, he first saw God's goodness inwardly. He imagined what God showed him. His faith formed a picture before his mouth formed words.

This is the pattern of Scripture. God told Abraham:

> *"...Lift up now thine eyes, and look from the place where thou art, ... For all the land which thou seest, to thee will I give it,"*
> (Genesis 13:14–15, KJV)

God said to Jeremiah:

> *"...what seest thou? ... Thou hast well seen: for I will hasten my word to perform it."*
> (Jeremiah 1:11–12, KJV)

God formed Ezekiel's vision of dry bones, asking him what he saw before commanding him to speak life over them, showing that vision preceded proclamation. (Ezekiel 37:1–10, KJV)

You cannot speak by faith until you see by revelation.

Faith begins with a picture: a whispered impression, a Scriptural promise, a vision God paints upon the heart. Then comes the declaration, and later the manifestation. Seeing is conception, when

God's vision takes form within the heart before it is ever visible in the world. Speaking is birth, as faith-filled words give voice to what God has planted within. Manifestation is growth, when what was conceived and spoken becomes evident through a transformed life, bearing fruit that both you and others can see.

Your Words Carry the Weight of Seeds

"Death and life are in the power of the tongue: ..."
(Proverbs 18:21, KJV)

Your words plant seeds, whether you intend them to or not. Some produce life; others decay.

Consider:

Words of fear plant anxiety.

Words of anger plant bitterness.

Words of doubt plant unbelief.

Words of faith plant strength.

Words of Scripture plant righteousness.

Words of worship plant peace.

Every sentence is a seed. Every seed produces something after its own kind. You decide which ones you sow.

Your heart is the field where seeds take root. Your words are the instruments that tend it, shaping growth toward faith or toward destruction. Nothing you say is neutral.

Speaking the Word in Agreement with God

Jesus said:

"…the words that I speak unto you, they are spirit, and they are life."
(John 6:63, KJV)

When you speak the Word of God under the leading of the Spirit, that same life flows through your confession. You are not shouting random positivity into the atmosphere. You are echoing eternal truth into temporary conditions. God confirms this truth in the book of Isaiah when He says:

"So shall my word be that goeth forth out of my mouth: It shall not return unto me void, …"
(Isaiah 55:11, KJV)

The Word builds what God desires and destroys what He opposes. It aligns what is crooked and strengthens what is weak. It corrects what is broken, heals what is wounded, and illuminates what is dark.

"The entrance of thy words giveth light; It giveth understanding unto the simple."
(Psalm 119:130, KJV)

When you speak in faith, you are not describing your situation; you are defining it according to God's truth. You are not reacting to what you see, but you are reinforcing what God has said. You are not commanding God; you are cooperating with Him.

Why Faith Must Speak

Faith that remains silent is faith that remains buried.

Salvation itself requires confession:

*"For with the heart man believeth unto righteousness; and with the mouth
confession is made unto salvation."*
(Romans 10:10, KJV)

Belief births righteousness, and confession births manifestation.
The order is intentional. God designed the heart to conceive faith
and the mouth to release it. If your faith never leaves your heart, it
never enters your world. If your belief never enters your mouth, it
never enters your life.

Speech is not optional in the kingdom of God. It is the expression
of faith, the agreement of the spirit, and the believer's cooperation
with the Holy Ghost.

Speaking as a Co-Laborer with God

Elias reminded his son of a powerful truth: We see first in the
Spirit, then we speak in faith, and then we watch God work.

This is not a presumption; it is a partnership.

It is the same pattern that carried Peter onto the water, led David
toward Goliath, and sent the apostles into the world.

Creation begins in the unseen. Agreement is formed in the mouth,
and manifestation follows obedient action. Faith speaks because it
trusts God's Word. Declaration matters because God's Word is
active and effective. Confession aligns the believer with what the
Kingdom is already doing.

You were created to speak God's Word in conscious agreement
with it, not as empty repetition, but as faith expressed through
understanding, obedience, and trust, even when your circumstances say otherwise.

Reflection and Practice

1. Reflection Question
Hidden seasons expose the depth of our trust in God. Ask yourself slowly: When nothing seems to be changing on the surface, what do my thoughts, words, and emotional responses reveal about what I truly believe God is doing underneath? Do I cling to His promise or collapse into impatience? Do I guard the seed or dig it up, looking for progress? Invite the Holy Spirit to show you where your faith rests securely and where it wavers. Let Him reveal the quiet places where trust needs strengthening.

2. Scripture Meditation
Read this passage aloud, with attention to each phrase:

"And he said, So is the kingdom of God, as if a man should cast seed into the ground; And should sleep, and rise night and day, and the seed should spring and grow up, he knoweth not how."
(Mark 4:26-27, KJV)

Then meditate on this instruction:

"Rest in the Lord, and wait patiently for him: …"
(Psalm 37:7, KJV)

Sit in silence for one full minute after reading. Let this truth settle into your heart: God is working, even when I cannot see how.

3. Prayer of Alignment
Lord, teach me to trust what You are doing beneath the surface. Quiet my impatience and steady my heart. Strengthen my surrender so that I choose Your pace rather than my own. Guard my words from doubt and fill them with faith. Help me honor the unseen work You are doing in my life. Remind me that hidden growth is still real growth and that Your timing is perfect. I rest in

what You are cultivating, even when I cannot measure progress. In Jesus' name, amen.

4. Action Step

Choose one specific promise from Scripture that speaks directly to a situation you are waiting on. Write it on an index card or record it in your phone. For the next three days:

Speak that promise aloud once in the morning.

Speak it again once at night.

You do this not to force the seed or accelerate its growth, but as an act of agreement with what God has already planted. Your voice becomes one of the ways you water what you cannot yet see.

5. Practice for the Week

Practice Ten Minutes of Stillness each day for the next seven days.

Set a timer for ten minutes.

Sit quietly with no music, no requests, and no agenda.

Begin by whispering, "Lord, I trust what You are doing beneath the surface."

Spend the remaining time resting in quiet availability before God.

Stillness becomes the spiritual greenhouse where hidden roots strengthen. By the end of the week, you may notice subtle but undeniable signs: peace returning before answers arrive, patience rising where frustration once lived, and a steady confidence that God's Word is working even when the ground looks unchanged.

Closing Prayer

"Father, thank You for showing me that Your Word carries life and power. Teach me to see what You see before I speak, and to say what You have already declared from Heaven.

Let my tongue become a tool of creation, not destruction, a vessel through which Your Spirit shapes my world. Guard my mouth from fear, doubt, and careless words. Let every sentence that leaves my lips carry faith, hope, and truth. Let my tongue become a tool of creation, not destruction, a vessel through which Your Spirit shapes my world. Guard my mouth from fear, doubt, and careless words. Let every sentence that leaves my lips carry faith, hope, and truth.

Help me to remember that I am made in Your image to reflect Your authority with humility, to speak Your promises with confidence, and to trust that Your Spirit performs what Your Word proclaims.

When silence feels heavy and progress unseen, remind me that You spoke light into darkness, and that the same light still moves within me.

May every thought align with Your heart, every word align with Your will, and every breath declare, 'Let there be light.' In Jesus' name, Amen."

Chapter 6

Life and Death in the Tongue

Morning mist rested low across the valley, soft as a veil, turning the vineyard into a tapestry of silver and green. Dew clung to every leaf, and the early sun cast long beams that made the vines shimmer like living rivers stretching down the hillside.

Elias stood on the porch with a warm clay cup in his hands, the steam carrying the scent of roasted barley. From this vantage point, he watched his sons tending their assigned rows. The land had awakened slowly that morning, as if reluctant to break the stillness. Birds flitted low between the vines, their wings brushing the air with gentle urgency, while somewhere beyond the hills a shepherd's horn sounded faintly, then faded.

Micah, now thirteen, worked with steady confidence, humming a psalm as he tied the young vines to their stakes. Each movement carried care; each knot was firm and deliberate. His hands moved with a rhythm that spoke of long observation and quiet learning. Elias noticed how Micah paused before each tie, checking the vine's direction, ensuring it would grow upward rather than twist back upon itself.

A few rows over, Jonah tugged at a stubborn weed. His small shoulders heaved with frustration as he muttered, "This soil is cursed. There are too many rocks here, and the rain never comes when it should."

Elias raised an eyebrow. He remembered saying things just like that years ago. Words spoken in weariness, unaware of the harvest they produced. He had learned, slowly and often painfully, that complaints had a way of rooting themselves deeper than weeds.

"Micah," Elias called. "Jonah, come here a moment."

Micah came at once, light-footed and eager. Jonah followed slowly, kicking clumps of dirt along the path, irritation written plainly across his face. Elias watched the contrast between them without judgment. Each son reflected a season he himself had lived through.

Elias gestured toward the bench. "Sit with me."

Jonah plopped down with a sigh. "If this is about my rows, I already know. They are the worst in the vineyard."

Elias set his cup aside. "Your rows are listening to you more than you realize."

Jonah frowned. "Listening? I am only saying the truth, Father. Look at the vines. Half of mine are withered."

Micah nudged him gently. "Mine are doing better. Maybe my rows listen better."

Jonah scowled, but Elias chuckled softly. "Ah, but both of you are speaking. The question is, what are you planting with your words?"

The door behind them opened with a soft creak. Hannah stepped out carrying a small tray with flatbread still warm from the oven, a bowl of olives, and a jug of cool honey-water beading with condensation. The morning light fell on her features, steady and bright, her presence filling the porch with calm strength. Elias felt, as he often did, that peace followed her wherever she went.

"Even farmers of faith need breakfast," she said as she handed each boy a cup.

Micah smiled gratefully. Jonah took a bite of flatbread and sighed. "This is better than rain."

Hannah laughed lightly and looked at Elias. "What lesson are you sowing this morning, husband?"

"Words," Elias said. "And how the vineyard listens."

Hannah tilted her head thoughtfully. "Then perhaps this is a morning for a story."

Together they walked to the fig tree near the vineyard's edge, where its wide branches cast generous shade. The valley spread before them, a sea of green rising toward the hills. The fig tree had stood there longer than any of them could remember, its roots deep, its fruit dependable year after year. Elias often thought of it as a silent witness.

Elias drew a circle in the dirt. "When our fathers came out of Egypt, the Lord told Moses to send twelve men to spy out the land He was giving them. They all saw the same land. Yet they did not all speak the same words."

Micah leaned forward. "Ten were afraid."

Jonah nodded. "The giants. They saw giants."

Hannah's voice softened as she continued the story. "Yes, they saw the giants, but their mistake was not what they saw. Their mistake was what they concluded about what they saw."

She settled beside them, the breeze tugging gently at her shawl. "The ten spies did not lie. The land indeed had giants. But fear shaped their words, and their words shaped an entire nation."

Micah shivered slightly. "They said, 'We cannot win.'"

Jonah whispered, "And the people believed them."

"Exactly," Hannah replied. "Fear spread through the camp like smoke in dry grass."

She paused, eyes distant, recalling the story as if she had stood among the Israelites herself. "Mothers clutched their children. Fathers panicked. People who had once walked through the Red Sea now trembled at the thought of tall men."

Then her voice deepened. "But Joshua and Caleb tore their clothes and cried out, 'Do not fear the people of the land. The Lord is with us.' They spoke faith, and faith carried a different harvest."

Elias nodded. "The Lord said to Moses, 'As you have spoken in My ears, so will I do.' The ten who spoke fear received fear's reward. The two who spoke faith received the land."

The boys sat in silence for a moment, the weight of the story settling. The vineyard rustled softly, leaves whispering against one another as though affirming the lesson.

Jonah swallowed. "So when I said things like 'my rows are cursed,' I am planting something?"

"Yes," Elias said. "Your words are seeds. Your heart is the soil. Your life is the harvest."

Hannah touched Jonah's chin lightly. "The tongue is the hand that sows."

Jonah lowered his eyes, considering this new responsibility. He glanced back toward his rows, seeing them now not as enemies but as listeners, waiting.

Micah whispered, "Then we should speak carefully."

Jonah nodded slowly, his eyes wider now. "Because what we say grows."

Elias smiled. "Exactly. Life and death are in the power of the tongue. Speak as one who expects God to rain on your faith, not on your fear."

Hannah reached for Elias's hand. "Then let us plant life together."

They bowed their heads beneath the fig tree. No long prayer followed, only a quiet agreement of the heart. The vineyard stood around them, rows upon rows of listening soil, and the morning light continued its slow work.

When the family rose, Jonah returned to his rows with a different posture. He knelt and gently cleared the weeds again, this time without complaint. Under his breath, barely audible, he spoke words of blessing instead. Micah resumed his work as well, his psalm rising more clearly now, carried on the breeze.

Elias watched them from the porch once more, his cup empty but his spirit full. He understood then that the vineyard was not merely growing grapes. It was growing sons. And beneath every spoken word, the soil remembered.

The Power of the Tongue

"Death and life are in the power of the tongue: And they that love it shall eat the fruit thereof."
(Proverbs 18:21, KJV)

"...for out of the abundance of the heart the mouth speaketh. A good man out of the good treasure of the heart bringeth forth good things: ... But I say unto you, That every idle word that men shall speak, they shall give account thereof in the day of judgment."
(Matthew 12:34-36, KJV)

Elias's lesson to his sons was not about grapes, soil, or weather. It was about the unseen atmosphere that words create. Every sentence spoken in the vineyard was a seed, and even the tone with which those words were spoken shaped what followed. Blessings and careless remarks alike carried effect beyond what the boys could yet perceive. The field, Elias said, responded to more than they realized.

Scripture teaches the same truth. Words are not mere sounds; they are spiritual seeds; every word plants either life or death, faith or fear, blessing or burden. Whether whispered, joked, muttered, or declared, nothing spoken is ever neutral. Everything bears fruit somewhere.

Jesus made it clear that people will give an account for their "idle words." Idle does not mean sinful; it means careless, empty, unintentional. Words that drift out of the mouth unguarded take root in places we did not intend. If good words build up, empty words tear down simply by neglect. Paul wrote:

"Let no corrupt communication proceed out of your mouth, but that which is good to the use of edifying, ..."
(Ephesians 4:29, KJV)

Edifying means building, and your words are always building something—either a house of peace or a house of fear, a field of blessing or a field of drought. This is why the tongue deserves spiritual attention.

Words Create Atmosphere

Every environment becomes the field where words take root.

At home, one word of encouragement can water the soul, while sarcasm or constant criticism can undermine a child's confidence or harden a spouse's heart. Elias understood this well. He told his sons that the vineyard yielded sweeter fruit when peace shaped their speech, and that complaining in the fields often led to diminished harvest and weary hands.

At work, speaking with gratitude honors God in the labor, while grumbling removes joy from the task. A worker who blesses his work invites God into it.

In worship, when believers speak praise aloud, the atmosphere shifts. Scripture teaches that God inhabits the praises of His people, and Heaven responds where His Word is honored. Confession tills the ground of the heart, thanksgiving waters it, and praise warms it, creating space for God's presence to dwell.

"But thou art holy, O thou that inhabitest the praises of Israel."
(Psalm 22:3, KJV)

The tongue tills the unseen. It can prepare the heart for God, or make it resistant to Him.

In private thought, the most hidden words of all still sow seeds. Internal murmuring chokes the Word of God before it reaches the heart. Silent thanksgiving prepares the heart to receive God's Word.

Creation itself responds to the words of the one stewarding it. Elias sensed this truth because God revealed it long before: mankind was given dominion through both hands and mouth. God spoke creation into being, and He made humans in His image. That means our speech carries spiritual consequence, not because we are divine, but because He is, and we carry His imprint.

Speech Reveals Alignment

Your words cannot change God's truth. His Word stands eternal and unshaken. But your words decide whether you are walking in agreement with that truth or resisting it. When your mouth speaks fear, doubt, resentment, or hopelessness, you are stepping out from under His promises, because His promises cannot be spoken in the language of unbelief. Jesus said,

> *"…the words that I speak unto you, they are spirit, and they are life."*
> (John 6:63, KJV)

Spirit-filled words produce life. Words devoid of the Spirit weaken the heart.

When a believer speaks Scripture in faith, the Holy Spirit moves upon those words just as He moved upon the waters in Genesis. Confession is not magic; it is agreement. It echoes what God has already said, so that your heart can anchor in truth while the Spirit performs His work.

For example, if you declare, "The Lord is my shepherd; I shall not want," while facing financial strain, you are not denying your need. You are stating that your need is not your master. God is. If you say, "By His stripes I am healed," while waiting for recovery, you are aligning your tongue with God's covenant rather than the fear rising inside you.

Words direct faith. Faith then directs the outcome.

Words as Spiritual Weeds or Spiritual Rain

Fear, doubt, bitterness, and murmuring are not harmless noises. They are weeds. Each one sinks roots into the soil of the heart. Weeds grow faster than fruit and choke life wherever they spread. They steal spiritual moisture, attract the drought of unbelief, and slowly suffocate joy, prayer, and hope.

Gratitude does the opposite. Praise calls down rain.

"Whoso offereth praise glorifieth me: And to him that ordereth his conversation aright Will I shew the salvation of God."
(Psalm 50:23, KJV)

Confessing Scripture invites God's intervention. Praising God when the ground looks dry calls forth spiritual rain. Elias's vineyard felt the change when the family blessed the land. In the same way, homes, marriages, workplaces, and churches feel the shift when God's people speak life.

Words Carry Kingdom Allegiance

When fear speaks, it often repeats the whisper that appeared in Eden.

"...Yea, hath God said, ..."
(Genesis 3:1, KJV)

The serpent's strategy begins with suggestion. Question God's intentions. Question His promises. Question His goodness. Doubt sprouts wherever that seed lands.

But when faith speaks, it works in cooperation with the Spirit of God. When a believer says, "God is faithful," heaven responds in agreement. When a father blesses his home, peace settles over it.

When a mother declares Scripture over her children, God's protection is invited, and His purposes are affirmed. Words become assignments in the spiritual realm, setting direction rather than merely expressing emotion. The tongue is not neutral; it is a gate through which heaven is given expression or opportunity is yielded to the enemy.

Idle Words Still Bear Fruit

Jesus warned that every idle word will be accounted for. Idle speech is not blatant or in-your-face sin; it is uncultivated speech—words spoken without faith, without attention, and without alignment. Such words drift like loose seeds in the wind and often land in places you never intended.

Many believers unintentionally curse their own lives. They say:

"I never get ahead." "This always happens to me." "I'm just tired of trying." "My kids will never change." "I'm not good enough."

These sentences are small, but they gather power as they repeat. They become the vocabulary of defeat. Over time, people believe the very things they have told themselves.

But the same principle works in the opposite direction, producing life instead of decay:

"God will provide."

"The Lord is my strength."

"The favor of the Lord surrounds me."

"I can do all things through Christ."

Words shape the direction of your future. What you speak today often becomes what you live tomorrow.

James compared the tongue to a rudder. It is small, but it controls direction. Your tongue is steering your life somewhere. If you change the direction of your tongue, you change the direction of your life.

Speak to the Field

When Elias taught his sons to speak blessing over the vineyard, he was teaching them how faith shapes the unseen. You do not wait for the field to improve before speaking to it. You speak to it so it can improve.

When your circumstances look barren, speak what God has promised, not what your eyes see.

Bless your home aloud:

As for me and my house, we will serve the LORD.

(Joshua 24:15, KJV)

Bless your work:

Establish Thou the work of our hands, Lord.

(Psalm 90:17, KJV)

Bless your church:

Where there is unity the Lord commands the blessing.

(Psalm 133:1–3, KJV)

Bless your children:

My children will walk in righteousness, and they shall be delivered.

(Proverbs 11:21, KJV)

Bless your mind:

My mind is stayed on the Lord, and He keeps me in perfect peace.

(Isaiah 26:3, KJV)

The tongue, trained by the Spirit, becomes the tool that tills the unseen field of life.

> *"A man shall be satisfied with good by the fruit of his mouth: ..."*
> (Proverbs 12:14, KJV)

Every word is a seed. Every seed produces fruit. Make sure the fruit you eat tomorrow comes from the words you speak today.

Reflection and Practice

1. Reflection

Your words reveal the atmosphere of your heart long before your actions do. Ask yourself carefully: What climate have my words been creating in my home, in my thoughts, in my relationships, and in my walk with God? Are my words planting faith or feeding fear? Are they building up or slowly corroding what God is trying to grow? Invite the Holy Spirit to show you truthfully and gently where your speech reflects trust and where it reflects unbelief.

2. Scripture Meditation

Read these verses aloud, slowly, letting each phrase rest on your spirit:

> *"Death and life are in the power of the tongue: And they that love it shall eat the fruit thereof."*
> (Proverbs 18:21, KJV)

"Let no corrupt communication proceed out of your mouth, but that which is good to the use of edifying, ..."
(Ephesians 4:29, KJV)

Meditate on this question:

What fruit have my words been producing? Sit quietly for one full minute and let the Spirit bring clarity.

3. Prayer of Alignment

Lord, set a watch over my lips and purify the atmosphere of my speech. Let my words agree with Your truth and carry the fragrance of life rather than fear. Uproot every habit of complaint, sarcasm, or careless talk. Teach me to speak blessing in my home, faith in my trials, and Scripture into my circumstances. Shape my heart so that the meditation within and the words spoken outwardly are pleasing in Your sight. Let my speech become a channel for Your peace and presence. In Jesus' name, amen.

4. Action Step

Choose one setting where your words carry significant influence: your home, workplace, marriage, friendships, or even your inner thoughts. Today, speak one deliberate blessing into that environment. Not a vague hope, but an explicit declaration anchored in Scripture.

Over your home:

"...but as for me and my house, we will serve the Lord."
(Joshua 24:15, KJV)

Bless your children:

"...the seed of the righteous shall be delivered."
(Proverbs 11:21, KJV)

Over your work:

"And let the beauty of the Lord our God be upon us: And establish thou the work of our hands upon us; Yea, the work of our hands establish thou it."
(Psalm 90:17, KJV)

Speak it aloud. Let the atmosphere hear you.

5. Practice for the Week

For the next seven days, practice "Verbal Weeding and Watering."

Each morning: Speak one promise of Scripture aloud to water the soil of your heart.

Each evening: Identify and uproot one negative pattern of speech you used that day, such as complaint, fear, gossip, frustration, self-criticism, or sarcasm. Confess it to the Lord and replace it with a spoken blessing or truth.

This rhythm will shift the atmosphere of your heart and home. You will begin to see peace where tension once lived, faith where fear once spoke, and a new steadiness in your confession. Your tongue is steering the direction of your life. This week, turn it toward life.

Closing Prayer

"Father, Forgive me for every careless word that has planted doubt in the soil of my life. Teach me to speak as You speak, words filled with Spirit and life. Let my tongue become an instrument of blessing, my home a field of faith, and my heart a vineyard that bears fruit worthy of Your name. Set a guard over my mouth, Lord, that every sentence sown would honor the One who redeemed me. In Jesus' name, Amen."

Chapter 7

The Voice of Faith

The storm had been building since morning, low clouds stacking over the hills until they looked like walls of charcoal rising against the sky. By midday, the wind shifted, carrying the heavy scent of rain and electricity. The birds grew restless along the fence line, fluttering from post to post, sensing what was coming.

Elias noticed the change long before the first rumble of thunder. He had learned to read the sky the way others read letters on a page. The air thickened. Sound traveled differently. Even the vineyard itself seemed to brace, leaves turning upward, vines pulling tight against their ties.

Storms were not new to him. But memory made this one heavier.

He wiped his hands on his trousers and stepped out of the vineyard shed, tightening the last rope around the shutter. The wood creaked beneath his grip as the wind pushed back, testing the latch.

"Micah, Jonah," he called. "Storm plan. Now."

The boys ran across the yard at once. They had rehearsed this many times. Micah gathered the loose baskets and rushed them under the porch. Jonah raced to bring in the goats and secure the feed barrels. Hannah moved steadily across the yard, collecting jars from the drying racks and covering the herb stands with cloth.

No one shouted. No one panicked. This was a household trained in readiness, shaped by seasons both kind and cruel.

Elias rechecked the sky. A dark shelf of cloud pressed forward like a great wave preparing to break. The horizon disappeared beneath it, swallowed whole.

The first gust slammed into the house, rattling the shutters.

"Inside," Hannah called to the boys as the wind sharpened. "Quickly."

The last of the chickens fluttered into the coop just as the wind turned fierce. Dust lifted from the road in spinning columns, racing toward the valley. Thunder rolled across the hills, low and heavy, as if the earth itself were groaning.

Elias and Hannah stayed outside a moment longer, moving in rhythm without speaking. He secured the final latch on the shed door. She gathered the last of the jars from the porch. Rain stung their skin in scattered drops, warning shots before the downpour.

When they stepped beneath the overhang, both were nearly breathless.

The rain began suddenly, each drop striking the ground like a thrown pebble. In seconds, the vineyard bent under the weight of it. Young vines bowed toward the earth, trembling under the sudden violence.

Water pooled in the furrows faster than the soil could drink it.

Hannah gripped her shawl tighter. "Elias," she said, raising her voice above the roar, "the young vines cannot endure this. Not again."

The words landed harder than the rain.

He stared out at the vineyard, watching the soil swell and darken. The memories rose without mercy. A season when hail stripped the leaves bare. Another time, floodwater drowned the roots before fruit could form; years of aching disappointment that had pushed his faith to the very edge.

"Not another season," he whispered, voice barely audible beneath the wind. "Lord, I cannot lose another season."

Thunder cracked across the sky, sharp and immediate, loud enough to make the porch boards tremble beneath their feet. The sound pulled his shoulders inward, the weight of old fear rising like an unwelcome shadow.

Fear had a voice. It always did.

You've prayed before.

You believed before.

And still the storm came.

Hannah stepped closer, placing herself squarely in his line of sight. Rain plastered loose strands of hair against her face, but her eyes were steady.

"Elias, look at me."

He turned.

"You taught our sons that the ground listens," she said. "Then let the storm listen too."

The words cut through him, not with accusation but with clarity.

He hesitated, caught between what he saw and what he believed. Between memory and promise. Between experience and truth.

Another thunderclap shook the valley, closer this time, as if daring him to choose.

Hannah took his hand and squeezed. "We know who commands the rain. Speak what you believe, not what you fear."

Her words struck something deep and ancient within him. A certainty older than disappointment. The same presence he had felt years ago in the Shepherd's voice. The reminder returned with force: faith was never meant to be silent in the face of challenge. Faith spoke.

Elias drew a steady breath, stepped off the porch, and stood in the rain.

Water streamed down his face and gathered in his beard. His clothes clung heavily against his skin. He felt exposed, small beneath the sky. But he also felt something else rising, steady and immovable.

Hannah stepped beside him, unwavering.

Together they lifted their voices.

"The Lord is faithful," Elias declared. His voice carried, decisive and deliberate. "This vineyard belongs to Him. He gave the seed, and He will protect the harvest. Father, we trust You."

The words did not beg. They aligned.

Hannah raised her hands toward the heavens. "Peace, be still," she said, her voice ringing with confidence. "Your Word says that even the winds and the sea obey You. We speak Your authority over this storm."

The rain continued for a moment longer, as if weighing the declaration.

Then something shifted.

The wind softened, losing its edge. Thunder rolled again, but farther away this time, retreating instead of advancing. The sheets of rain thinned into a heavy mist, then into a gentle fall that shimmered in the gray light.

The vineyard lifted slowly, vines relaxing back into place.

Elias lowered his hands. Hannah let out a breath she had been holding.

"It is not our words that move the mountain," she said quietly. "It is our faith agreeing with His."

Elias nodded, rain dripping from his lashes. "Heart and mouth," he said. "Belief and confession agree as one."

They stood together, soaked but steady, as the storm pulled back over the ridge and disappeared.

Silence returned gradually. Not the empty silence of danger passed, but the complete silence of order restored.

Inside the house, their sons watched from the window, eyes wide, breaths held. They would never forget this moment. Not because the storm stopped, but because of how their parents stood.

They saw unity.

They saw conviction.

They saw faith that spoke when fear demanded silence.

That night, after the house had settled and the rain had become only a memory tapping softly from the eaves, Micah spoke quietly.

"Father," he said, "were you afraid?"

Elias met his son's eyes. "Yes."

Jonah frowned. "Then why did you speak so boldly?"

Elias rested a hand on each of their shoulders. "Because fear listens too. And it must hear who is in authority."

The boys nodded, understanding more than they could explain.

Outside, the vineyard rested, roots drinking deeply from soil that had been spared.

It was the day they learned that storms do not bow to fear.

They bow to faith in agreement with God.

Faith's Two Voices

"...whosoever shall say unto this mountain, Be thou removed, and be thou cast into the sea; and shall not doubt in his heart, but shall believe that those things which he saith shall come to pass; he shall have whatsoever he saith."
(Mark 11:23, KJV)

"For with the heart man believeth unto righteousness; and with the mouth confession is made unto salvation."
(Romans 10:10, KJV)

Faith is never a silent reality. It begins in the heart as conviction, but it is completed on the tongue through confession. Heaven recognizes faith not by thought alone but by agreement between inner belief and outward declaration. Heart and mouth are the two instruments of faith, just as breath and sound are the two instruments of speech. One without the other leaves something essential unfinished.

This is why Jesus connected believing and speaking in the same breath. The heart holds the substance of what God has said, but the mouth releases that substance into the natural world. If the believed Word of God is the seed, confession is the act of planting that seed. In the same way, what is held within the heart does not benefit the world until it is drawn out and expressed through the mouth.

The Pattern of Scripture: Faith Speaks

Throughout Scripture, God reveals that the heart believes, and the mouth often responds in agreement. Though God works beyond human speech, faith is frequently given voice. Faith is the language of God's Kingdom.

Joshua and Caleb did more than think differently; they spoke differently. Surrounded by unbelief, they declared the land was theirs. Their confession separated them from a generation that died in the wilderness. (Numbers 13:30; 14:6–9, KJV)

David did not whisper hope before Goliath; he declared victory aloud while the giant still stood armed and mocking. His words created an atmosphere for God's intervention. (1 Samuel 17:45–47, KJV)

The centurion told Jesus, "Speak the word only, and my servant shall be healed." His confidence in the power of spoken truth caused Jesus to marvel and resulted in the healing of his servant. (Matthew 8:8–10, KJV)

Jesus Himself prayed aloud at Lazarus's tomb, thanking the Father before the miracle appeared, teaching us that thanksgiving is the sound of faith before manifestation. (John 11:41–44, KJV)

Faith, in every case, had two voices: inward conviction and outward expression. Neither was optional.

Heart Without Mouth Leaves Faith Dormant

There are many believers whose hearts hold truth that their mouths never release. They love God, trust Him, meditate on His promises, and even sense His guidance, yet their circumstances do not change because they never speak what they believe. Their faith is planted in private soil but never exposed to the light.

Silent faith is still faith, but it is unfinished.

Paul said,

> *"I believed, and therefore have I spoken;"*
> (2 Corinthians 4:13; cf. Psalm 116:10, KJV)

True belief leads to speech. Silence can be reverence, but it can also become paralysis. Faith must step from the hidden chamber of the heart into the open field of confession. Until it speaks, it remains potential rather than power.

Mouth Without Heart Leaves Faith Hollow

The opposite is also true. Some speak Scripture with confidence but without conviction. They declare promises but do not believe them. They repeat phrases but do not trust the God who spoke them.

Confession without heart agreement is noise. It is speech without substance. It is a shell without life.

Jesus warned against "vain repetitions." Words are not incantations; they are instruments of agreement. God does not respond to volume or repetition, but to genuine faith. An unbelieving confession is like a lamp with no oil. Outwardly, it appears capable of producing light, yet it lacks the power to illuminate.

When Heart and Mouth Agree, Heaven Responds

Faith is fully alive when the heart believes God's Word and the mouth proclaims what the heart believes. This is why Jesus emphasized agreement in Mark 11:23. The heart must be anchored in truth, and the mouth must be active. When the two align, Heaven recognizes its own echo.

Faith becomes a spiritual resonance. The Spirit of God moves where He hears the language of God.

This is the principle Elias and Hannah demonstrated during the storm. Elias believed God would protect their home, but he had grown weary. The storm challenged not only their vineyard but also their voice. His heart held the promise, but his mouth had grown silent. Hannah's words restored unity between faith within and faith expressed.

Their agreement made room for God to work; their unity released authority, and their confession redirected the storm.

This is not folklore; it is biblical law. Amos 3:3 asks, "Can two walk together, except they be agreed?" The same applies to the Spirit. He walks with those who speak what He says.

Why Faith Must Speak Aloud

There is spiritual power in spoken truth for several reasons grounded in Scripture:

1. Speaking Anchors Belief Inside You
Your own voice is the loudest voice your mind hears. When you speak God's Word, you reinforce your heart's confidence.

> *"So then faith cometh by hearing, and hearing by the word of God."*
> (Romans 10:17, KJV)

Hearing includes your own confession.

2. Speaking Resists the Enemy
Jesus resisted Satan by speaking Scripture, not by thinking it. The sword of the Spirit is not silent. "It is written" is spoken warfare.

> *"Then saith Jesus unto him, Get thee hence, Satan: for it is written, Thou shalt worship the Lord thy God, and him only shalt thou serve."*
> (Matthew 4:10, KJV)

3. Speaking Gives the Spirit Something to Move Upon

In Genesis 1, the Spirit was already moving over the waters, but creation did not take shape until God spoke. The Spirit was present, but the spoken Word gave direction, order, and form. God's Word did not summon the Spirit; it directed Him. In the same way, speaking in faith does not create power, but it gives God's already-present power something to move toward.

"...And the Spirit of God moved upon the face of the waters. And God said, Let there be light:"
(Genesis 1:2-3, KJV)

4. Speaking Aligns Your Atmosphere With Heaven

Words shape environments. Homes saturated with fear often cultivate anxiety, while homes saturated with truth cultivate peace. Scripture affirms this principle:

"The thoughts of the righteous are right: but the counsels of the wicked are deceit."
(Proverbs 12:5, KJV)

5. Speaking Releases What God Has Placed Within You

Jesus taught that what fills the heart eventually finds expression through the mouth:

"...for of the abundance of the heart his mouth speaketh."
(Luke 6:45, KJV)

The heart may receive God's Word, but the mouth is where that Word is released into life. What remains unspoken stays internal, shaping belief but not direction. When truth is spoken, it moves from conviction to expression, allowing faith to influence the world beyond the heart.

When Speech and Emotion Do Not Agree

Part of spiritual maturity is learning to speak truth even when feelings lag. Faith speaks from conviction, not emotion. Feelings shift like shadows, but the Word is stable. Faith does not pretend emotions do not exist. Instead, it refuses to allow emotions to define truth.

David often spoke directly to his own soul.

"Why art thou cast down, O my soul? and why art thou disquieted in me?
Hope thou in God: ..."
(Psalm 42:5, KJV)

He spoke to his emotions rather than from them, commanding his inner life to align with what he believed about God. Faith does not wait for the soul to feel right; it speaks truth until the soul submits to hope.

Faith talks to the soul until the soul submits.

Guarding the Mouth: The Discipline That Follows Faith

Speaking in faith requires guarding the mouth from agreement with darkness. Fear will present itself for confession. Doubt will reach for your tongue. Complaints will try to shape your speech. Discouragement will whisper its vocabulary. These are invitations to plant the wrong seed.

Elias warned his sons that careless words harden soil. Complaints thicken the atmosphere. Doubt dries the field. But when they blessed the vineyard, even the vines seemed to relax under the weight of peace. Words can change the environment even when circumstances have not.

Biblical Examples of Faith's Confession

The Scriptures are filled with men and women who learned the power of agreement between heart and mouth.

The Scriptures are filled with this pattern. Moses declared, "Stand still, and see the salvation of the Lord," before the Red Sea ever parted. Joshua spoke victoriously while Jericho's walls still stood. When Hannah failed to conceive, she prayed aloud until God reversed her barrenness. On many occasions, the prophets declared what was not yet visible until God brought it forth. When the angel Gabriel announced that Mary would bear the coming Messiah, she replied, "Be it unto me according to Thy word," and the Word made flesh entered the world. Their circumstances did not dictate their confession; their confession aligned them with what God was bringing to pass.

The Greatest Confession: Jesus Christ Himself

Romans 10 links confession not only to miracles but to salvation itself. The greatest miracle of all, eternal life, enters the believer's heart through faith that speaks. If the greatest miracle requires confession, so will the lesser ones.

God designed the mouth to be a gate for His work. When it opens in faith, Heaven's influence is given expression in the situation. When it closes in fear, what God intends is delayed, not denied.

When Elias stood beside Hannah in the storm, he discovered a truth many believers overlook. Sometimes you need another voice to help your own. Faith is strengthened in agreement. Hannah's confession stirred Elias's courage. Together they spoke what they believed: that God was present, that their home belonged to Him, and that peace could be spoken into chaos.

Their voices did not calm the storm because they were special. Their voices calmed the storm because they were aligned with God.

In the same way, every believer is called to release Heaven's truth into their world. You may not see the wind cease or lightning slow, but you will see peace return, strength rise, fear dissolve, and circumstances bend toward God's will. The authority is not yours; it is His. You are simply the voice that carries it.

Faith Speaks, Even When Conditions Do Not Change Immediately

Confession is not an instant manifestation. The farmer does not speak to the field once and expects a full harvest in the morning. He speaks continually because words are watering. They prepare the soil for the day the fruit appears.

Sometimes change begins within you long before it appears around you. The storm outside may continue for a time, but as you consistently confess God's truth, your inner life comes into alignment with Him. That alignment allows God's power already at work within you to shape your responses, decisions, and atmosphere over time, creating space for His purposes to be expressed outwardly according to His timing.

Faith's voice is steady. Faith's voice is patient. Faith's voice is persistent, trusting God to act in His time and in His way.

When Faith's Two Voices Are One

The mature believer reaches a point where heart and mouth do not contradict each other. What God says, the heart believes. What the heart believes, the mouth declares. What the mouth declares, the Spirit confirms. This is spiritual integrity. This is faith in fullness. This is in agreement with God.

The believer is transformed when heart and mouth speak the same language as Heaven. That agreement is what Jesus calls mountain-moving faith. Not because the believer is inherently powerful, but because the believer is aligned with God.

When your heart holds God's truth and your mouth releases God's truth, creation responds to the Creator's echo.

Reflection & Practice

1. Reflection Question
Faith has two voices: the heart and the mouth. Both must agree for the Spirit to move.

Ask yourself: Where in my life has my heart believed one thing, but my mouth spoken another? Have I prayed in faith yet spoken discouragement? Have I believed God's promise inwardly but confessed fear outwardly? Have I allowed weariness to silence what God has called me to declare?

Invite the Holy Spirit to show you any area where your heart and mouth need to be unified in surrender to God's Word.

2. Scripture Meditation
Read these verses aloud, slowly, letting the weight of them shape your inner posture:

"...That whosoever shall say ... and shall not doubt in his heart ... he shall have whatsoever he saith."
(Mark 11:23, KJV)

"For with the heart man believeth unto righteousness; and with the mouth confession is made unto salvation."
(Romans 10:10, KJV)

As you meditate, ask: What is God inviting you to believe in your heart and release with your mouth?

Sit with this question until a single phrase or conviction rises.

3. Prayer of Alignment

Lord, unite my heart and my mouth in Your truth. Remove every contradiction between what I believe and what I speak. Purify my confession so that my words carry faith, not fear; promise, not doubt; blessing, not complaint. Teach me to speak as one who belongs to You; calm in storms, steady in trial, and bold in obedience. Let my voice echo Heaven, not my emotions. Align me fully with Your Word. In Jesus' name, Amen

4. Action Step

Choose one area where your confession has been inconsistent: finances, health, marriage, children, calling, identity, or future.

Then do the following: Write down one sentence you have been saying that does not agree with God's Word.

Examples:

"Things will never change."

"I'm overwhelmed."

"I'm always failing."

Now replace it with a declaration rooted in Scripture. Speak the new declaration aloud three times today.

This is not performance. It is alignment. It is the heart and the mouth learning to walk together.

5. Practice for the Week

For the next seven days, practice Heart–Mouth Alignment.

Daily Morning Habit: Speak one promise aloud that you truly believe or are choosing to believe. Let your own voice strengthen your heart.

Daily Evening Habit: Review your day. Write down one moment when your confession drifted into fear, complaint, or negativity. Repent quickly, then speak truth over that moment.

By the end of the week, you will begin to notice something meaningful taking place. Your emotions will start following your confession. Your atmosphere will begin to change. Your confidence will increase. Your agreement with God will become instinctive rather than forced.

This is the maturity of faith: when heart and mouth speak the same language Heaven speaks.

Closing Prayer

Father, teach my heart and my mouth to agree. Let my words rise from faith, not fear; from trust, not striving. Forgive me for every confession born of doubt, and help me to speak what You have already spoken. Let my home, like Elias and Hannah's, be a place where faith has a voice and peace is its fruit. I believe Your Word is true. I confess that Your promises stand firm. Let Heaven hear my agreement, and let Earth reflect it. In Jesus' name, Amen.

Chapter 8

Guarding the Gate of the Mouth

"Set a watch, O Lord, before my mouth; Keep the door of my lips."
(Psalm 141:3, KJV)

The week after the storm, peace settled over the vineyard like a soft cloak. The ground steamed in the rising sun, and droplets clung to the vines like silver beads. Elias walked the rows each morning, touching the leaves as though checking the pulse of something precious.

Each step felt deliberate, reverent. He moved slowly, pausing often, letting his fingers brush the tender growth. The vines had endured more than they should have, yet they stood upright, strengthened rather than broken. Their resilience spoke louder than words.

"Not a single root lost," he whispered, breath thick with gratitude. "The Lord truly kept His word."

The words were not spoken to the vines alone. They were spoken to memory, to fear, to the lingering echo of seasons when storms had stolen more than fruit. This time, the harvest still lived.

From the porch, Hannah watched him with a gentle smile. She could always tell when his heart was quietly worshiping. Elias did not sing aloud, nor did he raise his hands. His praise lived in careful steps and thankful breath, in the way he handled what had been spared.

Micah and Jonah ran past her, jumping through the puddles that still lingered along the walkway, laughter stitching life back into the air. Their joy carried efficiently, unburdened, echoing against the walls of the house and spilling into the open morning.

For a time, the home felt completely whole.

There are moments like that, rare and fragile, when peace settles not because everything is finished, but because trust is resting in the right place. Hannah recognized it and did not rush it.

That evening, they gathered for supper. The smell of roasted herbs filled the house, and lamplight washed the table in a soft glow. Shadows danced along the walls as the flame flickered. The meal was simple, but it tasted rich with gratitude.

When the last plates were cleared, Elias reached for the scroll of Psalms. The parchment whispered softly as he unrolled it, the sound familiar and comforting. He read slowly, letting each word settle rather than rush ahead.

"Set a watch, O Lord, before my mouth; keep the door of my lips."

He looked up at his sons. "Do you know why David prayed this?"

Micah tapped his chin, thoughtful. "So he wouldn't say bad things?"

"Partly," Elias said. "But there is more. Even a good man can ruin a harvest with careless words."

The boys exchanged glances, considering the idea. Jonah shifted in his seat.

Hannah nodded. "Remember Zechariah, the father of John the Baptist? The Lord sent an angel to announce the promise of John's birth, but because Zechariah spoke in unbelief, God silenced him until the child was born."

Jonah's eyes widened. "God shut his mouth?"

"For protection," Hannah said. "A promise so precious cannot always survive a careless tongue."

Elias closed the scroll, thoughtful. "Powerful things must be guarded. Words especially."

Silence followed, not uncomfortable, but weighty. The boys felt it. Something important had been placed before them, like a seed carefully laid into the soil.

Later that night, a soft wind returned to the valley. Not a storm, only the restless whisper of a front passing through. Leaves rustled gently. The vineyard shifted and breathed.

Hannah stepped onto the porch, shawl pulled tight around her. The night air carried coolness and clarity. Elias joined her in the quiet, the familiar rhythm of companionship settling between them.

"Do you ever think," she said gently, "that words are the wind of the soul?"

Elias looked over at her. "What do you mean?"

"When we speak," she said, "we breathe out what is hidden inside. If our hearts are restless, our words become wild. But if our heart rests in God, our words will carry peace."

He considered this for a moment, then nodded. "So the gate we guard is not only our lips. It is our heart's first."

Before Hannah could respond, a sharp voice cut through the night.

"I told you it was a waste of time!"

Both turned toward the road. Two neighbors, Caleb and Orrin, were arguing as they walked past the vineyard fence. Their voices grew louder with each step, sharpened by frustration and pride.

"You always think you know best," Orrin snapped. "But look at the fields. You prayed, and the storms still came. Nothing changed."

Caleb spat into the grass. "At least I'm willing to say what's right in front of us. The crops are damaged. The ground is torn up. Better to speak the truth out loud than to talk like Elias does, as if words alone will fix it. Speaking faith doesn't stop storms."

Elias stiffened. He had not expected his name to surface in their quarrel.

Caleb's voice hardened. "He talks like everything will work out if you just keep blessing the sky. But storms don't obey men. And if he keeps teaching his boys to live in words instead of what's real, they'll break harder than his vines did last year."

Jonah stepped onto the porch, eyes wide. "Father… did you hear what they said?"

Elias felt the sting rise inside him. His first instinct was to answer the insult, to step onto the road and correct their words. He felt anger coil in his chest like a tightening rope. Old defenses surfaced quickly, rehearsed and sharp.

Then Hannah touched his arm.

"Remember the watch on your mouth," she whispered.

Micah appeared behind them, listening closely. "Father, what will you say back to them?"

The wind carried the faint echoes of Caleb and Orrin's argument down the road as they walked away, their voices dissolving into the night.

Elias closed his eyes and breathed. He felt the battle take place where no one else could see it, not between neighbors, but between reaction and obedience.

He looked at his sons.

"Nothing," he said at last.

Jonah frowned. "But they insulted you. And us."

Elias knelt to meet their eyes. "A man's insult cannot plant a harvest in my field unless I answer it with my own tongue."

Micah's brow furrowed. "So if you speak back, you plant their words?"

"Yes," Elias said softly. "Answering anger with anger is like watering weeds."

They stood quietly for a moment, the moon rising over the vineyard. The vines shimmered faintly, leaves stirring in the gentle breeze.

Hannah broke the silence. "Your father is choosing strength tonight. Sometimes silence is the loudest obedience."

The boys pondered her words without speaking. They were learning that restraint was not weakness, and quiet could carry authority.

Inside the house, the hearth crackled. A log split, sending sparks upward like fleeting words, bright for a moment, then gone. Elias watched them drift and disappear, their brief brilliance leaving no mark.

"Children," he said, "storms are not only made of weather. Some storms come through people's mouths. But just as we spoke peace to the sky, we must guard peace in our home."

Micah and Jonah nodded slowly, understanding more than they could say.

Hannah placed a hand over Elias's. "We keep watch together," she said.

And as the night settled around them, the breeze wound through the vines like a gentle reminder. Every word released into the world keeps traveling long after it leaves the mouth.

Some words build.

Some bruise.

Some carry life; others, loss.

And the wise learn to guard the gate.

Guarding the Gate of the Mouth

"For in many things we offend all. If any man offend not in word, the same is a perfect man, and able also to bridle the whole body. Behold, we put bits in the horses' mouths, that they may obey us; and we turn about their whole body. ... Even so the tongue is a little member, and boasteth great things ..."
(James 3:2–5, KJV)

"Set a watch, O Lord, before my mouth; Keep the door of my lips."
(Psalm 141:3, KJV)

The lesson from Elias's household is one Scripture has declared for centuries: the tongue may be small, but it governs the direction of entire lives.

A vineyard is shaped not by a single moment of weather, but by the atmosphere it is exposed to over time. Words shape the atmosphere of the heart in the same way. They create the climate in which growth either flourishes or withers. And just as a sudden frost can damage even a healthy vine, one unrestrained moment of speech has the power to wound what love has spent years nurturing.

When Elias had corrected Jonah sharply in the past, the issue was not that the correction itself was wrong. It was the tone, the timing, and the lack of restraint that made the truth harder to receive. Jonah would pull back. Micah would react. The entire atmosphere of the home would shift.

What changed in this moment was restraint. Hannah's gentle intervention restored peace without escalation. She became the thermostat rather than the thermometer, guiding the home's climate back toward calm and strength.

James 3 explains why moments like this matter so deeply. Just as a bit guides a horse and a rudder steers a ship, the tongue has the power to direct the course of a believer's life. Both the bit and the rudder are small, yet they exert tremendous influence over direction. In the same way, speech may seem minor, but it shapes outcomes far beyond its size.

James also warns that the tongue carries destructive potential. A single spark can set an entire forest ablaze. So too, unrestrained words can ignite patterns that damage relationships and grieve the Spirit. What directs can also destroy, which is why mastery of speech is inseparable from spiritual maturity.

A believer who masters his speech can master his direction. A believer who refuses to be restrained will eventually drift into patterns that grieve the Spirit and damage relationships.

Restraint Is a Fruit of the Spirit

Galatians 5 teaches that self-control is part of the fruit of the Spirit. This includes restraint and wisdom in speech.

A Spirit-filled life is defined not merely by powerful speech, but by well-governed speech. It is characterized not just by bold words, but by wise words; not only by declarations of faith, but by disciplined responses.

Scripture emphasizes this repeatedly:

> *"He that keepeth his mouth keepeth his life: ..."*
> (Proverbs 13:3, KJV)

> *"...be swift to hear, slow to speak, slow to wrath:"*
> (James 1:19, KJV)

> *"Whoso keepeth his mouth and his tongue Keepeth his soul from troubles."*
> (Proverbs 21:23, KJV)

Jesus Himself demonstrated restraint. When falsely accused before Pilate, He spoke nothing. His silence carried more authority than any defense could have. Pilate marveled, not because Jesus was powerless, but because His power was under perfect control. This is restraint in its purest form: authority that chooses silence until the Spirit permits speech.

Ungoverned Speech Leeches Spiritual Strength

Proverbs warns that death and life flow from the tongue. This is not poetic exaggeration. It is a spiritual reality.

Scripture teaches that:

Idle words matter (Matthew 12:36-37 KJV).

Complaining invites destruction (1 Corinthians 10:10 KJV).

Grumbling distorts the heart (Philippians 2:1 -15 KJV).

Corrupt talk grieves the Spirit (Ephesians 4:29-30 KJV).

Idle, in this context, does not mean humorous or casual. It refers to speech that is unrestrained, unfiltered, and disconnected from faith. Idle speech tears down trust, multiplies anxiety, and contradicts the truth of Scripture.

A single spark can set a forest ablaze. One careless phrase can darken a family's atmosphere. One unguarded moment can sow the seeds of insecurity in a child or doubt in a spouse.

We see this pattern taking shape in Elias's home. In moments of pressure, words began to reveal what was stirring beneath the surface. Frustration gave rise to careless speech. Reactivity edged out discernment. Even correction, when sharpened by emotion, landed harder than intended. Yet gentle restraint restored peace, inviting the heart of the Father back into the room.

The entire household shifted because of words. What James teaches about the tongue became visible in that moment. A few restrained sentences brought peace, while unspoken reactions prevented further harm. Direction changed without force, volume, or argument. This is the wisdom James describes in James 3: words may be small, but they steer outcomes, shape atmosphere, and reveal maturity. In that quiet exchange, the power of disciplined speech proved greater than the power of reaction.

Guarding the Gate: A Biblical Pattern

To guard the gate of your mouth is not repression. It is reverence. It is giving the Holy Spirit the authority to filter speech before it becomes sound.

Guarding the gate includes:

1. Guarding the Heart First

> *"...for out of the abundance of the heart the mouth speaketh."*
> (Matthew 12:34, KJV)

The tongue reveals what the heart conceals. Speech is the overflow of the inward condition. Changing the mouth requires tending the heart.

If the heart is restless, words will be sharp. If the heart is bitter, words will be cold. If the heart is fearful, words will be defensive. But if the heart is yielded, softened, and filled with Scripture, the mouth becomes a well of life.

This is why God so often addresses the heart before He addresses behavior. The condition of the inner man determines the direction of every word that follows. When the heart is kept in communion with God, speech becomes less reaction and more reflection of His presence.

2. Giving the Spirit Veto Power

"...the Spirit of truth, is come, he will guide you into all truth:"
(John 16:13, KJV)

Guidance from the Spirit is not limited to our actions; it also includes our speech. Every believer should know the gentle restraint of the Spirit. The quiet inner check before speaking, the pause, the warning, the sense of Do not say that.

Those who honor that restraint grow in wisdom, while those who ignore it often regret their words.

Learning to heed that inward prompting is part of spiritual maturity. The Spirit's restraint is not meant to silence truth, but to protect it from being spoken at the wrong time, in the wrong tone, or from the wrong place. When believers learn to listen before they speak, their words carry clarity, grace, and lasting fruit.

3. Pausing Before You Release Words

"He that hath knowledge spareth his words: ..."
(Proverbs 17:27, KJV)

The pause is not hesitation; it is discernment. One breath of restraint can prevent regret that lingers far longer than the moment itself. In that brief space, emotion loosens its grip and wisdom is given room to speak. The pause allows truth to surface before impulse takes control, turning reaction into response. Often, what is withheld for a moment is transformed into something far more life-giving when it is finally released.

Pausing creates space for the Holy Spirit to purify intention. It is often the split second that turns a sharp correction into a gentle one, a reactive comment into a healing one, and a harmful remark into a gracious reply. In that pause, the heart is given time to catch up with truth, and wisdom is allowed to lead instead of emotion. What is delayed for a moment is often delivered with far greater clarity and grace.

Scripture captures this wisdom clearly:

"A word fitly spoken Is like apples of gold in pictures of silver. As an earring of gold, and an ornament of fine gold, So is a wise reprover upon an obedient ear. As the cold of snow in the time of harvest, So is a faithful messenger to them that send him: For he refresheth the soul of his masters."
(Proverbs 25:11–13, KJV)

4. Speaking Only What Aligns With Scripture

"Let the word of Christ dwell in you richly..."
(Colossians 3:16, KJV)

When Christ's words dwell in your heart, the Word of God becomes the filter for your speech.

If what you intend to say contradicts Scripture, the Spirit will restrain you. If it aligns with truth, He empowers it.

What makes a believer's speech effective is not personality, eloquence, or intelligence, but alignment with God's Word.

When Christ's words dwell in your heart, the Word of God becomes the filter for your speech. If what you intend to say contradicts Scripture, the Spirit will often restrain you with a quiet check. Effectiveness comes not by forcing words into the moment, but by yielding your speech to truth. When your words agree with God's nature, God honors them, and your voice becomes a vessel for His purposes rather than a reaction to circumstance.

What the Story Teaches Us

Elias's restraint did not come from perfection, but from humility. He chose not to answer offense with offense, and that choice protected the atmosphere of his home. Hannah's gentle words reinforced that restraint, steadying the moment and modeling wisdom for their sons.

This is how families recover—not through flawless speech, but through guarded speech; not by never faltering, but by responding rightly when pressure comes.

The most significant power of the tongue is not in how forcefully it speaks, but in how carefully it does.

The most significant power of the tongue is not found in forceful speech, but in submitted speech. A mature believer learns that words must pass through discernment before they are released. When anger rises or pressure mounts, thoughts no longer move directly to the mouth; they are filtered through truth.

Wisdom pauses to ask, What does God say about this?

Faith responds by agreeing with His Word, not reacting from emotion.

This kind of speech creates an atmosphere where God's presence is not resisted but welcomed; where words spoken in the home do not grieve the Spirit, thoughts rehearsed in the mind do not oppose Him, and the heart remains tender enough to receive His quiet instruction.

Guarding the gate of the mouth is not a small discipline. It is spiritual warfare. It is stewardship of the inner climate. It is the practice that sustains faith under pressure. And it is the mark of a life that desires not only to speak to God, but to speak in agreement with what He has already spoken.

Reflection and Practice

1. Reflection
Every word you speak shifts the atmosphere toward life or toward death, toward peace or toward tension.

Ask yourself honestly:

Which area of my life suffers most from unguarded speech?

Is it my home, my marriage, my children, my workplace, or my inner thought life?

Where do impatience, sarcasm, frustration, or careless words slip out most easily?

In what moments do I hear the Spirit caution me, yet override that prompting with my own words?

Identify the environment that needs your restraint the most. Let the Holy Spirit reveal it clearly and gently.

2. Scripture Meditation
Sit with these passages and read them slowly. Allow them to examine your tone as much as your vocabulary.

"Set a watch, O Lord, before my mouth; Keep the door of my lips."
(Psalm 141:3, KJV)

"He that keepeth his mouth keepeth his life: ..."
(Proverbs 13:3, KJV)

"Even so the tongue is a little member, and boasteth great things..."
(James 3:5, KJV)

Ask the Spirit, "What do these verses reveal about the stewardship of my words?"

Remain with the question until conviction gives way to clarity.

3. Prayer of Alignment

Lord, place Your hand on my mouth and Your peace upon my heart. Teach me the beauty of restraint. Let my words carry gentleness when I want to react, wisdom when I want to rush, and truth when I feel pressure. Remove every phrase driven by fear, pride, or frustration. Let the atmosphere of my home, my relationships, and my inner world reflect Your presence. Make my speech a well of life rather than a spark of destruction. Guard my lips and purify my tone. In Jesus' name, amen.

4. Action Step

For the next twenty-four hours, practice The Holy Pause before responding to anything significant.

Pause for a deliberate two seconds, then ask yourself:

Is what I am about to say constructive or destructive?

Does it reflect God's Word or my emotions?

Would the Holy Spirit release this word or restrain it?

If the answer is unclear, choose silence or gentleness. This simple discipline reshapes the climate of your conversations.

5. Practice for the Week

Strengthen the discipline of guarded speech through this daily rhythm:

Morning: Pray Psalm 141:3 aloud before speaking to anyone.

Midday: Replace one emotional phrase with Scripture.

Examples:

Instead of "I can't handle this," say,

> *"...The LORD is the strength of my life;"*
> (Psalm 27:1, KJV)

Instead of "Nothing ever changes," say,

> *"The Lord will perfect that which concerneth me: ..."*
> (Psalm 138:8, KJV)

Instead of "I am overwhelmed," say,

> *"Thou wilt keep him in perfect peace, ..."*
> (Isaiah 26:3, KJV)

Evening: Ask yourself, Where did I speak life today, and where did I complain? Write one sentence of repentance and one of blessing for tomorrow.

By week's end, you'll feel a calmer heart and a gentler atmosphere; the fruit of guarding your words.

Closing Prayer

"Lord, teach me the holy weight of words. Let my speech carry peace, not pressure; truth, not haste. Set a watch before my mouth, and make my heart the first gate You guard. Forgive the words that have wounded, and heal the fruit they bore. May silence become wisdom in me, and Your Spirit shape every sentence. In Jesus' name, Amen."

PART III

FROM WORD TO WORK: ACTING IN FAITH

Faith that is planted and spoken is now moving toward full fruition. Every promise of God seeks a willing vessel through which it can become visible. The Word does not dwell in us merely to comfort or instruct; it calls us to move.

In the hidden place of the heart, faith is conceived. Upon the lips, it is confessed. But through the hands, it is completed. This is where revelation meets obedience, where belief steps into motion, and where the invisible begins to yield fruit.

> *"Even so faith, if it hath not works, is dead, being alone."*
> (James 2:17, KJV)

Faith that is received and believed begins its work inwardly, often unseen. God's Word first takes root in the soil of the heart, forming conviction long before any visible evidence appears. When that inward faith is spoken in agreement with what God has planted, it does not begin the work, but cooperates with it.

Some promises grow quickly, producing fruit within a season. Others take time, developing deep roots before anything visible emerges. In the same way that corn bears fruit in the year it is planted, while an apple tree may require years before it yields, God determines both the pace and the process. Whether hidden or visible, growth is already taking place. This is what it means for faith to come to full fruition.

When God speaks, His Word always calls for a response. Scripture consistently shows that miracles unfold through obedient action. "Stretch forth thy hand." "Go, wash in the pool." "Fill the waterpots with water." "Rise, take up thy bed, and walk." The Word carries power, but obedience gives it expression.

Faith is not proven in the comfort of prayer alone; it is demonstrated in the courage to act. The heart that truly believes cannot remain still; it must build. It must move, give, forgive, and begin again.

In this section, we follow Elias as he learns that revelation without motion produces frustration, but revelation joined with obedience yields fruit. He rises to rebuild what was lost, takes steps that test his trust, and walks in a rhythm of daily faith that transforms his life from within.

Each stage reveals this divine pattern in motion:

Word → Belief → Speech → Action → Fruit

This is the movement of heaven on earth, the journey from promise to performance. As Jesus said

> *"If ye know these things, happy are ye if ye do them."*
> (John 13:17, KJV)

You have learned to prepare the soil of the heart and to speak in faith. Now you will learn to walk it out, to live as one whose every step is shaped by what God has spoken. The season of waiting has ended. The season of building has begun.

Chapter 9

Rise and Build

"But be ye doers of the word, and not hearers only, deceiving your own selves."
(James 1:22, KJV)

The vineyard had entered its quiet season. The vines, once bending under the weight of their harvest, now curled at their tips. Their leaves browned along the edges, the sweetness of the last harvest lingering faintly in the cool air. Elias stood at the edge of the property, watching the morning fog drift low across the hills like a soft veil. The year had been good, better than any since the famine, yet something restless stirred in him.

Peace had returned to the land, but rest had not yet settled in his spirit. He inhaled slowly, letting the scent of damp earth and dying leaves fill his lungs. There was no urgency in the vineyard now. No pressing harvest. No storm on the horizon. And yet the quiet itself seemed to ask something of him.

Beyond the fig tree and the stone wall, half hidden in shadow, stood the old workshop. Its roof sagged under the burden of many winters. Moss filled the cracks in its foundation. The beams that once glowed with fresh cedar were gray and bowed. Elias had walked past it for years with the quiet concession that its time was finished.

It had been easier to tend what was growing than to confront what had been neglected.

But something was different that morning.

A thin shaft of light pierced the mist and fell across the broken roof. Dust lifted through the gap in the planks, rising like smoke from an altar. Elias stopped mid-step. His breath caught, and the world seemed to still around him.

A memory surfaced, sharp and sudden. The voice of the Shepherd from the dream, the One who had led him through valleys and set a table before him.

"Tend what I give you."

The words had carried him through famine, through storms, through seasons of waiting. Now they returned with fresh weight.

He sensed that same voice again, not ringing in his ears, but stirring in the deep inner place where God speaks to the obedient.

"Rise and build."

The command was simple. That made it heavier.

Elias turned toward the house. Hannah stood on the porch, shawl wrapped around her shoulders, watching him with a calm knowing in her eyes. She did not ask what troubled him. She had learned to recognize the look of summons on his face.

"You heard it too," Elias said softly.

She nodded. "Every morning I pass that place, I feel the same stirring. As if something still breathes there."

Elias exhaled slowly. "We do not have the time, or the timber."

"Neither did those who rebuilt the temple," she replied. "Yet God told them to go up the mountain and bring wood. He provided when they moved, not before."

He looked again at the workshop, at its decay and its promise. "It has been years since I touched a beam. The boys are busy with the vines. And winter is almost upon us."

Hannah stepped closer, her voice gentle but firm. "The season does not decide obedience. God speaks. We respond."

Her words settled on him with the weight of truth. She had grown in the rhythms of heaven as profoundly as he had. Together they had learned that when God stirred a heart, delay was disobedience disguised as caution.

That afternoon, Elias opened the shed and pulled out his tools, each one coated in a thin film of dust. The handles felt unfamiliar in his hands at first, heavier than memory suggested. Micah and Jonah hurried to help, their faces bright with expectation.

They carried the tools to the workshop. Each step stirred the scent of old cedar and memory. Elias heard echoes of his father's laughter, the rasp of saws on fresh wood, the early days when he believed every work of his hands mattered.

Inside, light streamed through the gaps in the roof, creating columns of gold in the dimness. Cobwebs hung like threads of time. A broken yoke lay half buried beneath straw. Elias knelt beside it and ran his hand over the splintered wood. He remembered when that yoke had been new. When strength and promise still felt limitless.

"Lord," he whispered, "if You are asking me to rebuild this house, show me where to start."

A breeze slipped through the wall, stirring the dust at his feet. He could almost hear the voice of Haggai echo in the air: "Consider your ways. Build the house, and I will take pleasure in it."

Elias rose, shoulders firm, eyes steady. "Then we begin."

Work started that evening. Micah hauled timber from the storehouse. Jonah gathered nails, ropes, and tools. Hannah prepared warm bread and kept a lamp burning at the door until the final light left the sky.

At first, the work was slow. They replaced two planks, then reinforced a single roof beam. The wood resisted them, swollen with age and weather. Elias felt the strain in his arms, the ache in his shoulders.

But with each board lifted and each nail driven, strength returned to his hands. His movements regained the confidence of an earlier season. Muscle memory awakened, guiding his grip and stance as though time itself were yielding.

And with each motion, he felt the quiet hum of worship rising.

The rhythm of obedience had become the rhythm of praise. Each hammer strike, each sweep of sawdust, each breath of effort carried the same meaning as prayer.

They were building, but they were also worshiping.

As they worked, unseen eyes watched. Not the eyes of men, but of spirits. Some whispered doubt, hoping to thin Elias's resolve. Others stood in reverent stillness, bearing witness to obedience. The air would thicken at times, pressing against him with an invisible resistance.

Each swing of the hammer answered the pressure with faith. Each cut of the saw pressed back against the heaviness that had lingered since the loss. The rhythm of the work steadied his breathing, turning effort into offering. This was not labor done in striving, but in agreement.

The workshop became a place of quiet devotion. Wood yielded beneath obedient hands, and with it, something hardened in Elias began to soften. The work itself became prayer, unspoken, embodied, faithful. Every measured cut, every careful joint, declared trust in a God who restores through obedience, not haste.

It was not only wood being shaped. It was the unseen battle between doubt and devotion. And devotion was winning, not through words alone, but through faithful hands moving in step with God's plan.

Elias felt the resistance most in his thoughts.

It is too late.

You are too old.

This place is too broken.

But he refused to yield.

Scripture had taught him that resistance must be met with persistence. James had written, "Submit yourselves to God. Resist the devil, and he will flee from you."

Not to flee at the first prayer.

Not to flee at the first step.

But flee when resistance becomes steady.

So Elias kept going. He pressed through every whisper. He answered every doubt with another moment of obedience.

By the seventh day, the heaviness was gone. The valley echoed only with the sound of holy labor, as if the land itself welcomed the work being done upon it.

One evening, as the sun lowered behind the vineyard, Elias

stepped back to look at the workshop. The new beams glowed gold. The roof no longer sagged. The doorway stood straight and ready.

It was far from finished, but it was alive again.

Hannah came beside him and rested her hand on his arm. "It is beautiful," she said.

"It is obedience," he replied.

Inside, a soft wind moved through the room while the world outside held its breath. Fresh cedar filled the air, steady and grounding. A holy presence settled there, as though the moment itself had been set apart.

Elias closed his eyes and whispered, "Lord, this house is Yours."

As twilight deepened, the lamplight from their home flickered in the window of the workshop. Two lights glowing in agreement: faith and work, side by side, each reflecting the other.

The work had begun.

But the purpose had only just awakened.

The Movement of Obedience

*"This people say, The time is not come, the time that the Lord's house should
be built... Consider your ways."*
(Haggai 1:2-7, KJV)

The book of Haggai reveals a truth as old as covenant itself: obedience is the doorway through which God manifests His pleasure and presence.

Israel had finally returned from exile. They were back in the land God promised, surrounded by evidence of His mercy. But although they were restored geographically, their priorities had drifted spiritually. The temple lay in ruins while they poured their energy into building their own homes.

They were not rebellious. They were distracted. They were busy. They were comfort-driven. They were waiting for a "better time."

Their words were polite, even spiritual-sounding: "Not yet, Lord. Maybe later."

But delayed obedience is a window into the heart. It reveals hesitation where faith should be, self-preservation where surrender should rule.

God's answer was not condemnation, but invitation:

*"Go up to the mountain, and bring wood, and build the house; And I will
take pleasure in it, and I will be glorified, saith the Lord."*
(Haggai 1:8, KJV)

Notice the sequence:

Go up.

Bring wood.

Build the house.

I will take pleasure in it and be glorified.

God's pleasure comes after our movement. Not because we earn His favor, but because obedience positions us under His blessing.

Revelation Demands Movement

Just as in Haggai, the same pattern played out in Elias's story. The workshop had been abandoned for years—not because Elias despised it, but because he assumed its season had ended. He passed it day after day, scarcely noticing its collapse. But when the Lord whispered, "Rise and build," the revelation demanded a response.

Revelation always calls for motion. No one grows spiritually by collecting instructions they never act on.

James stated it clearly:

"Draw nigh to God, and He will draw nigh to you..."
(James 4:8, KJV)

This is divine reciprocity. We move toward Him, and He moves toward us. He initiates by speaking; we respond by obeying; He answers by revealing more.

Elias took the first step. He picked up tools he had not touched in years. He called his sons. He swept out the dust. He lifted the first broken board.

And Heaven responded.

At first, the work was slow, two planks, then a beam. But each act of obedience stirred the unseen realm. Resistance rose, not because Elias was off course, but because he had stepped onto contested ground.

Scripture explains this spiritual pushback:

"Submit yourselves therefore to God. Resist the devil, and he will flee from you."
(James 4:7, KJV)

First submission: aligning with God's direction. Then resistance: pushing back against every whisper that contradicts it.

Elias learned what all believers eventually can understand: obedience must outlast opposition. The enemy does not flee at our first act of faith. He flees when resistance becomes a way of life.

This is why James teaches that faith grows only when obedience joins it:

"Even so faith, if it hath not works, is dead, being alone."
(James 2:17, KJV)

"Seest thou how faith wrought with his works, and by works was faith made perfect?"
(James 2:22, KJV)

Faith becomes "perfect," not flawless, but mature through movement. Through action. Through risk. Through the steady rhythm of "yes, Lord" repeated day after day.

Obedience Is the Bridge Between Promise and Fulfillment

The great heroes of Scripture model the same pattern. God did not wait for circumstances to change before calling them to move; He spoke, and they responded in obedience. Their faith was not proven by what they believed privately, but by what they did publicly in response to God's Word. In every case, movement preceded manifestation, and obedience became the pathway through which God's promises were fulfilled.

Noah started building the Ark before the rain. Long before a single cloud gathered, he obeyed a word that contradicted everything he could see. Day after day, he labored in faith, constructing an ark on dry ground while the world around him carried on unchanged. His obedience was not fueled by evidence, but by trust in the God who had spoken. The rain did not validate Noah's faith; his obedience did.

"By faith Noah, being warned of God of things not seen as yet, moved with fear, prepared an ark to the saving of his house; by the which he condemned the world, and became heir of the righteousness which is by faith."
(Hebrews 11:7, KJV)

Abraham walked before he saw. God did not give him a map, a timeline, or confirmation along the way. He gave him a word, and that word required movement. Abraham left what was familiar and stepped into uncertainty, trusting that obedience would lead him where sight could not. The inheritance was not revealed first; it was discovered along the path of faith.

"By faith Abraham, when he was called to go out into a place which he should after receive for an inheritance, obeyed; and he went out, not knowing whither he went."
(Hebrews 11:8, KJV)

Moses lifted his rod before the sea parted, obeying God's command while the path ahead was still closed. The waters had not yet moved, and the threat behind them still pressed close; nothing in nature suggested escape, yet obedience required action before explanation. The raised rod became a declaration that God's Word was more reliable than what Moses could see. Only after he moved did the waters respond, and the path opened where faith had already stepped. What appeared reckless in the eyes of fear became wisdom in the hands of obedience. God met movement with a miracle.

"And the Lord said unto Moses, Wherefore criest thou unto me? speak unto the children of Israel, that they go forward: 16 But lift thou up thy rod, and stretch out thine hand over the sea, and divide it: and the children of Israel shall go on dry ground through the midst of the sea."
(Exodus 14:15–16, KJV)

The widow prepared vessels before the oil flowed, collecting empty jars in obedience to God's instruction. Only after she made room did the provision multiply.

"Then he said, Go, borrow thee vessels abroad of all thy neighbours, even empty vessels; borrow not a few. 4 And when thou art come in, thou shalt shut the door upon thee and upon thy sons, and shalt pour out into all those vessels, and thou shalt set aside that which is full."
(2 Kings 4:3–4, KJV)

Peter stepped out before the water supported him, responding to Jesus' invitation while the storm still raged. Faith did not remove the waves; it taught him where to stand. The miracle was not in the calming of the sea, but in the sustaining power beneath his feet once he obeyed the word spoken to him.

"And Peter answered him and said, Lord, if it be thou, bid me come unto thee on the water. And he said, Come. And when Peter was come down out of the ship, he walked on the water, to go to Jesus."
(Matthew 14:28–29, KJV)

Obedience is the bridge between revelation and manifestation.

Elias's workshop became that bridge. Every obedient swing of the hammer was worship. Every board lifted was an intercession. Each night, Hannah lit the lamp. It was a quiet agreement with the Word God had spoken.

Colossians declares:

> *"And whatsoever ye do, do it heartily, as to the Lord, and not unto men;"*
> (Colossians 3:23, KJV)

It was not the workshop's beauty that pleased God. It was Elias's surrender. His willingness to say, through labor, sweat, and persistence, "Lord, Your Word governs my actions."

Isaiah captured this promise:

> *"If ye be willing and obedient, ye shall eat the good of the land:"*
> (Isaiah 1:19, KJV)

Elias dedicated the workshop with a whisper, "Lord, this house is Yours." But in truth, he was dedicating far more. He was dedicating his life to a place where obedience becomes instinct, where revelation leads to immediate action, and where every movement is offered as worship to God.

This is the movement of obedience. It is not dramatic. It is not always emotional. It is quiet, steady, and sacred. And Heaven always honors obedience.

Reflection and Practice

1. Reflection
God has given you something specific in this season, a calling, an assignment, a prompting, or a step to take. Ask yourself honestly: Where in my life am I delaying obedience, even though I know what God has already said?

Have I been treating God's instruction as something to admire rather than act on? Where have I been waiting for certainty instead of obeying the next clear step? Take a moment to reflect quietly before God. Consider what He has already spoken to you, an instruction, a prompting, a calling, or an assignment you recognize as His. Ask yourself how you have responded. Have you treated His words as something to admire, or something to act upon?

As you sit with these questions, invite the Holy Spirit to bring clarity, not condemnation. Let Him name plainly any place where obedience has stalled. Then write down one area where you already know what God has said, but you have not yet moved in response.

2. Scripture Meditation

Sit with these verses until they impress themselves on your will, not just your understanding.

> *"Even so faith, if it hath not works, is dead, being alone."*
> (James 2:17, KJV)

> *"Seest thou how faith wrought with his works, and by works was faith made perfect?"*
> (James 2:22, KJV)

> *"But be ye doers of the word, and not hearers only, deceiving your own selves."*
> (James 1:22, KJV)

Read them aloud slowly. Then ask the Holy Spirit: "Where have I mistaken knowing for obeying? Where have I called delay 'wisdom' when it is really fear?" Let Him show you one place where faith must become motion.

3. Prayer of Alignment

Lord, You have spoken to me before, and I confess that I have not always moved when You called. Forgive me for admiring Your Word while resisting Your instruction. Today, I surrender hesitation, excuses, and the fear of getting it wrong. Teach me to be a doer of the Word and not a hearer only. Show me the next step and give me the courage to take it, even when I cannot see the whole path. Let my life reflect obedience rather than delay. Make my obedience worship, and let every step please You. In Jesus' name, amen.

4. Action Step

Name and obey one concrete step. Return to the instruction or vision you most connected with as you read this chapter: A business to begin, a conversation to have, a ministry to serve in, a book to write, a habit to rebuild, a relationship to restore, a financial step to take, or a discipline to resume.

Do three things:

Write a sentence beginning with, "The Lord has already shown me to…"Finish it with clear, specific language.

Ask, "What is the smallest obedient step I can take in the next twenty-four hours?" Do not plan the whole journey. Focus only on the next faithful step.

Do that step. Make the call. Send the message. Block out the time. Start the outline. Obedience is the doorway God uses to confirm His Word.

5. Practice for the Week

For the next seven days, practice Faith-in-Motion Journaling using this simple rhythm:

Morning: Pray, "Lord, show me one act of obedience You are asking of me today." Write it in one short sentence.

Afternoon: Treat that step as holy. When delay whispers, "Do it later," answer with:

> *"Even so faith, if it hath not works, is dead, being alone."*
> (James 2:17, KJV)

Then move.

Evening: Ask, "Did I move when God spoke today?" If yes, thank Him for the grace to obey. If no, repent without shame and write, "Lord, by Your grace I will obey tomorrow."

Repeat this for a whole week and watch faith turn into movement.

Closing Prayer

"Father, You are the Master Builder, and I am the work of Your hands. Forgive me for the times I have delayed obedience or built my own plans while neglecting Yours. Teach me to rise and develop where You have called me, to move when You speak, and to work as one who builds with eternal purpose. Let every hammer blow and every work of my hands become worship to You. Take pleasure in the house I built for Your name. In Jesus' name, Amen.

Chapter 10

Faith Without Works Is Dead

"Even so faith, if it hath not works, is dead, being alone. Was not Abraham our father justified by works, when he had offered Isaac his son upon the altar? For as the body without the spirit is dead, so faith without works is dead also."
(James 2:17, 21, 26, KJV)

Winter pressed in early that year. Frost laced the vineyard each morning, turning the rows into rivers of white that melted by noon. The newly restored workshop stood firm against the cold, its cedar walls glowing softly in the dim light, a quiet testimony of obedience carved into wood and time.

Each morning, Elias paused before stepping inside. He found himself lingering longer than necessary, studying how the light struck the grain of the wood, how breath fogged briefly in the air before disappearing. The workshop had become a marker in his days, not just of labor completed, but of something awakened.

Inside, the hearth crackled. Tools hung neatly along the wall. The air smelled of sawdust, fresh bread, and warm oil from the lamps.

To anyone passing by, the workshop looked complete. Finished. Blessed.

But heaven was not finished with Elias.

He stood at his bench one morning, running his hand over a plank of olive wood. He traced each line in the grain like someone reading a familiar story. The wood reminded him of the paths his family had walked these past seasons: hard ground softened, seeds buried, storms rebuked, faith spoken, and obedience lived. Each line was a testimony.

He thought of the years when his hands had gone idle, not from laziness, but from discouragement. Seasons when hope had narrowed to survival rather than calling. Now his hands moved again, steady and sure, and the difference felt holy.

He lifted the chisel, preparing to cut the first notch for the workshop's back doorframe, when the impression of a whisper broke his concentration. It was not audible, not something he could have explained aloud, but a quiet inward prompting that made him pause.

"Now fill it."

Elias froze. The chisel hovered in the air. His breath caught mid-inhale. He set the tool down slowly and glanced around the room.

"Fill it?" he murmured. "With what, Lord?"

He had assumed the work was finished because the building now stood strong. He had measured obedience by completion, by structure restored, by effort expended. But the whisper pressed deeper, a conviction rather than a command.

"You have built the house. Now let it serve."

Elias took a slow breath. There it was again, the familiar tension between faith and reason; the place where logic paused, and obedience was asked to step forward without full explanation.

"Serve what purpose?" he asked, though the question came more from hesitation than ignorance.

No audible answer came, but the impression grew with clarity. The workshop was not meant to be a monument to obedience, but a vessel of purpose. A place where the blessings of God could flow out, not simply be admired. A place of work, generosity, teaching, and refuge for others in ways he could not yet see.

The realization unsettled him.

It was easier to build than to open. Easier to restore wood than to invite people. Easier to measure planks than to steward what God might bring through the door.

He rested both hands on the bench and bowed his head. "Lord," he whispered, "I do not know how to hold what You are asking."

Later that evening, he told Hannah what he sensed.

She was kneading bread by the hearth, the warm light catching the gentleness in her face. Her hands moved with quiet rhythm, pressing and folding, shaping something simple into nourishment. She paused, pressing the dough flat beneath her palms.

"Fill it?" she echoed. "With what the Lord gives, of course."

Elias sighed, rubbing his temples. "It is a beautiful house now, Hannah. But I do not know how to begin this next thing. What if I heard wrong? What if it is beyond us?"

She leaned her weight on the counter and looked at him with a mixture of tenderness and boldness. "The Lord does not ask for expertise; only obedience. You taught the boys that faith is not complete until it is put into action. This is simply the next step."

Her words landed gently but firmly, like a seed placed in willing soil.

He smiled despite himself. "You have been listening too well."

"Always," she said softly.

That night, Elias lay awake longer than usual, listening to the wind move along the eaves. The workshop stood just beyond the window, its presence felt even in the dark. He realized that obedience often comes in layers. God rarely reveals the full design at once. He gives just enough light for the next step.

And the next step now was not building, but making room.

The next morning, the family gathered in the workshop. Elias, Hannah, Micah, and Jonah stood in the center as the morning light filtered through the window, illuminating the space with quiet expectancy.

"We will begin with what we already have," Hannah said.

There was no ceremony, no grand declaration; only movement.

She handed the boys jars of oil, bundles of wood, and sacks of grain, and they carried them to the shelves along the back wall. Elias brought in extra tools and laid them out carefully. Micah swept the floor, his movements deliberate. Jonah stacked blankets near the hearth and mended what needed mending.

As they worked, Elias watched his sons closely. They did not ask why. They obeyed, trusting the process as they had learned to do. Something in his chest warmed at the sight.

It did not look like much, but it was the unmistakable first movement of faith, faith expressed through action.

By dusk, they were finished. The workshop, now furnished and warm, felt different. Prepared. Expectant. Not full, but ready.

That very night, a sound echoed through the cold: a low knock on the outer gate.

Elias lifted a lantern and stepped outside. The air bit sharply against his face. Two travelers stood there, weary and half-frozen, their cloaks stiff with ice. Behind them, their donkey slumped beneath the weight of worn packs.

"Please," one of the men said, breath trembling, "the storm caught us on the ridge."

Without hesitation, Elias opened the gate wide. "Come in. Warm yourselves."

They entered the workshop with wide eyes, as though they had stumbled into a place built just for them. Hannah handed them bowls of stew and warm cloths. Jonah led the donkey to shelter. Micah piled wood onto the fire. Within minutes, the room filled with light and life.

The travelers ate slowly, hands shaking as warmth returned. Their shoulders lowered. Their breathing steadied. Peace settled over them like a blanket.

Later, as they slept by the hearth, Elias stood beside Hannah and whispered, "The moment we made room, the Lord filled it."

Hannah rested her head lightly on his shoulder. "Faith does not wait until we have nothing left," she said softly. "It moves while there is still something in our hands."

Elias let the truth settle inside him. The workshop was no longer rebuilt. It was doing what God intended. It was serving.

The next day, a widow from the town arrived, carrying a broken stool and a look of quiet desperation. Elias repaired it for her without charge, his hands moving with renewed purpose. A week later, a young couple came needing counsel for their struggling marriage. Hannah sat with them by the fire, praying with quiet authority.

More people came in the weeks that followed, drawn not by announcement but by the unmistakable scent of God's peace.

Some came with broken tools. Some with weary hearts. Some came to sit in the warmth.

The workshop had become a living testimony.

And Elias understood something he had never seen so clearly before:

Faith that stops moving is faith that begins dying.

Faith that continues obeying becomes faith that multiplies.

One evening, as he cleaned his tools in the warm glow of the hearth, he whispered, "Lord, faith is not finished until it gives. Until it serves. Until it moves outward."

The fire crackled softly, as if amen echoed in the flames.

Outside, snow fell in gentle sheets over the vineyard. The world lay quiet, wrapped in winter's stillness.

But inside the workshop, obedience had already begun its next season.

A season of giving.

A season of service.

A season of living faith.

A season where every small act of obedience became the seed of something greater.

Faith That Moves

"...so faith without works is dead also."
(James 2:26, KJV)

Faith does not mature by collecting revelation. Faith matures by responding to revelation.

Knowledge alone never transforms the heart. Insight alone never completes obedience. Revelation becomes life only when it becomes movement.

This is why Scripture emphasizes not simply believing, but obeying. James does not argue that our actions replace faith. Instead, he teaches that action proves that faith is alive. Belief is conceived in the heart. Obedience brings it into visible form.

When God gives instruction, obedient movement becomes worship. In Elias's story, the workshop did not become a house of faith when the final board was nailed into place. It became a testimony the moment Elias opened its doors, trusting that what God had stirred within him was meant to be lived out, not merely admired. Faith did not mature because the work was completed, but because obedience moved from intention to visible action in alignment with God's purpose.

Abraham believed God's promise, but Scripture teaches that his faith was "made perfect" through obedience, as his belief was carried into action from the moment God spoke until he reached the altar (James 2). At that point, God stopped his hand, showing that faith had already reached its full expression.

Peter believed Jesus' voice on the water, but his faith came alive the second his foot left the boat (Matthew 14). Throughout the Scriptures, revelation always demands a response.

"Shew me thy faith without thy works," James challenges, *"and I will shew
thee my faith by my works."*
(James 2:18, KJV)

To understand why faith must move, let's consider two patterns
that appear in the lives of believers. The first follows the rhythm
of Scripture while the second quietly suffocates faith with hesitation.

Scenario A: Faith in Motion

Obedience That Walks With God:
A believer receives a vision from God. A calling.A dream. A promise whispered in prayer. A task that carries His fingerprints.

They cannot see the whole path, but they take the next obedient
step. They pray, "Lord, where do I begin?" and God answers not
with a detailed map of every outcome, but with a single step. He
reveals just enough for obedience, inviting them to move forward
in trust rather than certainty.

They make room for God's provision, like the widow who gathered borrowed vessels so the oil could multiply (2 Kings 4).

They build with what is already in their hands, like Nehemiah rebuilding the walls of Jerusalem despite opposition (Nehemiah 6).

They obey one instruction at a time, like Abraham leaving his
home without foreknowledge of his destination (Genesis 12).

They stand firm against discouragement and spiritual opposition,
as James instructs believers to submit to God and withstand the
enemy (James 4).

They keep their confessions aligned with Scripture, as Paul teaches
that belief and confession work together unto salvation and life
(Romans 10).

And they trust God to establish the work of their hands, as Moses prayed for the Lord's favor to rest upon faithful labor (Psalm 90).

With each step they take, God directs the next.

This is faith moving. This is faith working. This is faith partnering with God.

God breathes on obedient motion. He multiplies what is surrendered. He strengthens what is offered. He directs what is dedicated.

> *"…without faith it is impossible to please him:"*
> (Hebrews 11:6, KJV)

Faith is a prerequisite to pleasing God, not because He is hard to satisfy, but because faith is the posture that creates space for Him to work.

Scenario B: Faith Without Motion

Good Intentions Without Obedience:
Another believer receives a vision from God.

A promise.

A calling.

A dream that clearly bears Heaven's imprint.

They believe it.

They treasure it.

They rehearse it.

But they do not move.

Instead, familiar assumptions keep them still:

"If God wants this done, He will do it without me."

"If it is meant to happen, it will happen automatically."

"I don't want to make a mistake, so I'll continue to wait."

"If the vision is truly from God, He will drop it into my lap."

"What if this isn't God at all, but just my own thoughts?"

So they wait, but not in the biblical sense.

Biblical waiting does not mean inactivity or avoidance.

It seeks God.

It listens for clarification.

It responds in obedience.

Faith that refuses to move is not humility; it is hesitation disguised as wisdom. God often confirms His voice not before obedience, but through it. As steps are taken, clarity follows. Direction sharpens. The path becomes visible under obedient feet.

This waiting becomes passivity disguised as spirituality.

It is often reinforced by teaching that does not agree with Scripture:

"Effort means unbelief." "All striving is flesh." "If God wills it, you do nothing, and He does everything."

But Scripture contradicts this pattern every time.

Noah built the ark. Moses lifted the rod. Joshua marched around Jericho. Ruth gleaned in the fields. Nehemiah rebuilt the wall. The early church prayed, served, preached, gave, traveled, and suffered.

Nowhere in Scripture does God hand someone a finished vision. He gives the word and requires obedience.

This passive believer loves God. They are sincere. They believe the promise.

But without movement, faith becomes theory, not testimony.

This believer suffers with the tormenting thought: "Why is God not fulfilling His promise to me?" But the truth is that nothing is broken in God's promise. What is missing is obedience.

Just as Jesus taught in the parable of the talents in Matthew 25, unused gifts do not fade because God changed His mind, but because His servants refused to act.

This is not a condemnation. This is clarity.

God gives the word. We provide the obedience.

Where Both Paths Converge

Both believers heard from God. Both received revelation. Both carried something holy.

But only one moved.

And Scripture declares the reality:

> *"Even so faith, if it hath not works, is dead, being alone."*
> (James 2:17, KJV)

Dead faith is not unbelieving faith. Dead faith is unmoving faith.

Faith that is alive is proven through consistent obedience.

And when even a small step of obedience is taken, God responds.

He breathes upon it. He strengthens it. He multiplies it. He confirms it. He surrounds it with grace. He draws near.

Because God delights in those who move at His voice.

It is not our perfection that pleases Him. It is our participation.

When Elias opened the doors of his rebuilt workshop, he did not simply finish a project. He honored a revelation. He answered a call. He offered obedience in motion.

And Heaven moved with him.

This is the faith that moves mountains, where knowing what God says becomes the foundation, and doing what He says becomes the expression.

Reflection and Practice

1. Reflection
Take some time to reflect in God's presence and ask yourself: Where in my life have I treated a word from God as something to admire instead of something to obey? Think about specific things, not generalities:

A conversation you know you should have had.

A step of generosity you felt prompted to take.

A project, ministry, business, or creative work, He stirred in you.

A habit to lay down or a discipline to pick up. Which scenario describes me right now?

Scenario A: Faith in motion

Taking steps without seeing the full path.

Scenario B: Faith on pause.

Be honest. God already knows. This question is for your transformation.

2. Scripture Meditation

Read these verses aloud several times until they begin to reshape your will and align your desires with God's.

"Even so faith, if it hath not works, is dead, being alone."
(James 2:17, KJV)

"But wilt thou know, O vain man, that faith without works is dead? Was not Abraham our father justified by works, when he had offered Isaac his son upon the altar? Seest thou how faith wrought with his works, and by works was faith made perfect?"
(James 2:20–22, KJV)

"The steps of a good man are ordered by the Lord: and he delighteth in his way."
(Psalm 37:23, KJV)

Sit with both the tension and the promise: Faith without movement is dead, yet every obedient step delights the Lord.

3. Prayer of Alignment

Lord, You know every promise You have spoken over my life. You know where I have obeyed and where I have delayed. I confess that I have often waited for perfect conditions, full clarity, or complete confidence before moving. Today I bring You both my faith and my feet. Show me where I have buried what You gave me. Reveal where fear, passivity, or confusion has replaced obedience. I surrender the lie that You will do everything without me. You give the Word, and I will obey. Give me the courage to take the next step, even if it feels small. Let my faith be seen not only in what I say, but in what I do. Order my steps and delight in my way as I move at Your voice. In Jesus' name, amen.

4. Action Step
Identify and act on one delayed obedience this week.

At the top of a blank page, write: "What have You already told me to do, Lord, that I have not yet done?"

Wait in silence and list what comes to mind: forgiveness, a conversation, a job application, a ministry step, a skill to develop, a budget to create, a book to begin, a sin to confess.

Ask, "Which one are You asking me to move on first?"

Circle that one. Then write one specific step you can take in the next 24 – 48 hours.

Do that step as worship, not performance.

As you move, say, "This is faith in motion. God meets me as I obey."

5. Practice for the Week
Live as a Scenario A believer for the next seven days through this simple rhythm:

Morning: Surrender the Day. Pray, "Lord, show me today's step of obedience."Read Hebrews 11:6 aloud. Ask, "Where can I say yes to You today?"

Midday: Check Your Posture. Pause for two minutes. Ask, "Right now, am I living Scenario A or Scenario B?" If you sense hesitation, pray, "Lord, I step out of delay and into obedience," and take one small action before the day ends.

Evening: Review with God. Ask, "What step of obedience did I offer today?"Thank Him for movement, repent where needed, and write, "By Your grace I will obey tomorrow."

By week's end, you will notice obedience feeling more natural, hesitation losing strength, and the gap between hearing and doing beginning to shrink. That shrinking gap is where faith becomes testimony.

Closing Prayer

"Father, You call me not only to hear, but to act. Forgive me for every time I've believed yet failed to move. Renew my courage to obey You even when the way is unclear. Let my faith live through my hands, my giving, my service, and my love. Teach me to open doors where You have spoken, to make room for others, and to let my life become a living testimony that faith still works. In Jesus' name, Amen."

Chapter 11

Walking It Out

"If ye abide in me, and my words abide in you, ye shall ask what ye will, and it shall be done unto you. Herein is my Father glorified, that ye bear much fruit;"
(John 15:7–8, KJV)

Spring arrived softly that year, not with the violence of sudden storms or the roar of melting rivers, but with slow breaths of warm wind that carried the scent of new beginnings. The vineyard woke first, unfurling timid leaves like tiny green hands stretching toward the sun. The hills followed, shedding winter's gray for a rising blush of color.

The earth seemed to exhale after months of holding its breath. Frost had loosened its grip weeks earlier, yet the land had waited, quietly, cautiously, before committing itself to color again. Elias noticed that. Growth had not rushed back. It had returned with humility.

In years past, spring had come abruptly, rain beating against shutters and swelling the river until it roared through the valley. This year, the change felt deliberate. Almost reverent. As though the soil itself had learned something through winter and was now responding with measured confidence.

Elias walked the rows each morning, his fingers brushing lightly across the leaves. He examined the tendrils curling upward, grateful for every sign of life. Bees moved from blossom to blossom in a soft hum that sounded strangely like a song of blessing.

He did not count the clusters yet. It was too early for that. Instead, he studied the way each vine reached, whether it leaned too heavily on its support, whether a branch had grown ambitious too quickly. He had learned that fruit revealed itself in time, but direction revealed itself early.

Once, Jonah had asked why he touched nearly every vine.

"To remind myself that they are not numbers," Elias had answered. "They are living things entrusted to us."

The bees did not hurry. They drifted lazily, almost ceremonially, from blossom to blossom. Their hum rose and fell with the breeze, a low, steady tone that settled something deep in Elias's chest. He had once heard a traveler describe blessing as something dramatic and unmistakable. But standing there among the gentle stirrings of spring, Elias thought blessing often sounded more like this: quiet, constant, unassuming.

The workshop stood behind him in full strength now, its cedar beams polished by months of work and warmth. The windows glowed each night with lamplight. The shelves were no longer empty. The hearth rarely cooled. The building breathed with purpose.

There had been a time when that building felt more like a question than an answer. Elias remembered the first beam he set in place, how the wind had pressed against it as though testing his resolve. There were evenings he had returned from the field too weary to lift another tool, yet he had done so anyway, whispering small prayers between hammer strikes.

Now the structure stood firm. The scent of cedar had deepened into something richer with age. The grain of the wood had darkened where hands passed daily, as if obedience itself left polish behind.

At night, when the lamplight shone through its windows, travelers on the distant road sometimes slowed. The glow did not shout for attention, but it invited. It spoke of honest work and of warmth waiting inside.

Inside, Hannah kneaded dough on the wide table, her sleeves rolled to her elbows, flour clinging to her hands. The rhythm of her work was steady and peaceful. Micah sat by the window, repairing a neighbor's broken tool. Jonah hummed a psalm as he sorted jars of preserved figs, arranging them carefully on the shelf.

Hannah pressed the dough forward, folded it back, turned it, and pressed again. The movement had become part of her strength without strain. She had once told Elias that kneading reminded her of prayer.

"It feels like working something through until it softens," she had said.

Micah tested the handle he was securing, adjusting the fit with patient precision. His brow furrowed in concentration, yet there was satisfaction in his posture. The tool belonged to old Thomas down the hill, who had injured his wrist. Micah had volunteered to repair it before being asked.

Jonah paused in his humming long enough to hold a jar toward the light. "Mother, this one sealed perfectly," he said.

"Then place it in the back," Hannah replied. "The strongest foundations hold the longest."

Jonah nodded solemnly, as if entrusted with a sacred task.

It was a home filled not only with labor, but with life.

Life lingered in the small interruptions, the soft scrape of chair legs, the quiet laughter when flour dusted Jonah's sleeve, the way Micah cleared his throat before asking a question he already knew the answer to. There was space here for mistakes and for correction, space for growth and for grace.

Elias stepped into the doorway and paused, leaning his shoulder against the frame. He watched them for a moment, a quiet smile on his face, breathing in the scents of bread, oil, and cedar.

For a heartbeat, he said nothing. He observed. The sight before him carried weight. Years ago, he had feared that obedience might cost him comfort. Now he saw that obedience had constructed something far deeper than comfort. It had built stability.

"This place didn't come together because of our hands," he said softly. "It came together because our hearts learned to obey."

The words did not carry pride. They carried remembrance.

Hannah looked up, brushing a strand of hair from her cheek. "It builds itself because the Builder has not left," she replied.

There was no hesitation in her voice. She did not speak as one guessing at truth, but as one who had tested it.

Elias nodded, the truth of her words settling deep within him. He realized that nothing about this moment had arrived suddenly. Every act of obedience in past seasons, every small step of faith spoken or lived, had quietly led them here. This was not a triumph that announced itself with noise or spectacle. It was a blessing that had accumulated slowly and now rested gently, steady and sure.

He remembered the first time he chose obedience when it cost him something visible. The loss had stung. The outcome had seemed uncertain. Yet looking back, he could trace a line from that moment to this one, a straight, steady line.

That evening, as the sun burned low over the hills, the family gathered around the table for supper. The room glowed with the warmth of the fire. Bread steams when torn. The grape juice in their cups caught the light like garnet stone.

Jonah tore his piece of bread too quickly and burned his fingers. Micah laughed softly, then passed him a cloth. Hannah poured oil into a shallow dish, the golden surface rippling gently.

They bowed their heads to pray, and Elias spoke, voice steady and full.

"Lord, You have proven Yourself faithful. Every seed has found its season. Every promise has taken root. What You have grown in us, let it never stop bearing fruit."

His words lingered in the room even after the prayer ended. No one rushed to eat.

When they lifted their heads, Jonah squinted thoughtfully. "Father," he said, "the vineyard is full. The workshop is full. Does that mean the Lord is finished with us?"

The question held innocence and sincerity.

Elias chuckled gently. "The Lord is never finished, son. Full branches still need pruning."

Micah frowned a little. "But pruning means cutting," he said. "Why would God cut something off that is good?"

The fire shifted in the hearth. Outside, the wind brushed softly against the walls.

Elias rose from his chair. "Come," he said. "Let me show you."

They stepped outside into the softness of twilight. The vineyard glimmered under the rising moon, leaves like trembling silver in the breeze. He led them to a branch heavily laden with clusters of grapes.

The weight of the fruit pulled the branch downward, almost humbly. The vine had done its work well, perhaps too well.

"See how this branch bends?" Elias said. "If I leave every cluster, it will break under its own blessing. It is carrying more than it can sustain. But if I trim it, it grows stronger, and its fruit grows sweeter."

Jonah reached toward the grapes but stopped short, as if unsure whether touching them might alter the lesson.

Hannah joined them, laying a gentle hand on his arm. "The same is true of us," she said. "God trims our lives, not to harm us, but to shape us for more fruit."

Jonah ran his fingers over the heavy branch. "So pruning is not punishment?"

"No," Elias said. "It is mercy in disguise. Our obedience plants the fruit, but God's correction is what protects it."

Micah absorbed that quietly. He had felt correction before. The thought that it might be protection softened something in his expression.

The boys nodded slowly, letting the picture sink in. Above them, the stars blinked awake, one by one, as the night deepened.

For a long moment, they stood together in the quiet of the vineyard. The rows stretched around them like a great congregation, whispering in the wind.

The breeze shifted direction, and with it came a subtle chill that did not belong entirely to the evening.

Elias drew a deep breath and whispered, "The glory of the latter house will be greater than the former."

Hannah smiled beside him. "And in this place," she said gently,

"He will give peace."

The family lingered beneath the stars, content and rooted. There was a depth in the air, a heaviness of blessing, as though heaven itself rested over the land.

Yet as Elias looked out across the vineyard, his eyes narrowed. Far beyond the last row, near the tree line, a faint stirring moved in the shadows. The wind shifted. The air tensed.

It was not loud. It was not visible long enough to name. But it was enough.

Something flickered at the edge of his spirit, a sense he had learned not to ignore.

He exhaled slowly.

"The harvest is good," he said quietly. "But the work is not finished."

Hannah followed his gaze, her expression softening with understanding. She knew the look on her husband's face, the one that appeared whenever the Spirit whispered of things yet to come.

"This is only the beginning," she said.

Elias nodded. "Yes. And whatever comes next, we will walk it out as we always have. One step of obedience at a time."

The vineyard rustled in agreement, as though creation itself heard the promise.

And somewhere in the unseen places of the spirit, the next chapter began to stir.

The Endurance of Obedience

Faith without endurance remains inspiration without transformation. It rises quickly but fades just as fast. Scripture shows repeatedly that God's greatest work in His people does not happen in moments of excitement, but in the slow rhythm of daily obedience. Glory may begin a journey, but endurance establishes it.

Joshua was not told to meditate occasionally, but to meditate on "this book of the law" day and night (Joshua 1:8, KJV). Jesus did not call His disciples to visit Him at their convenience, but to abide in Him continually (John 15:4, KJV). David did not say, "Your Word I glanced at," but "Thy word have I hid in mine heart" (Psalm 119:11, KJV).

This divine pattern remained true in Elias's life. The workshop was not rebuilt because of one strong moment of inspiration. It stood because he returned each day, even when he felt tired, uncertain, or unseen. Endurance turned revelation into structure and calling into reality.

God's work in a believer is seldom formed in a single moment, but is most often shaped through faithful, godly habits. He accomplishes much through steady obedience over time.

How God Designed Us to Grow

Endurance in obedience is not merely spiritual. It matches the way God designed the human mind, body, and soul to learn.

Think of any skill you have ever developed: a trade, a craft, a musical instrument, leadership, business, parenting, marriage, or ministry. The first attempt often felt unfamiliar and awkward. Confidence did not arrive immediately; it grew through repetition. In the same way, God's design for steady and sustained growth is reflected in how life itself develops:

Muscles strengthen through repeated resistance.

Memory deepens through repeated exposure.

Mastery forms through repeated practice.

Wisdom matures through repeated experience.

Spiritual maturity grows in the same way. What we observe in human development reflects something deeper. This is not merely human psychology; it is divine design. Isaiah describes this steady layering of truth as:

> *"...precept upon precept, line upon line;"*
> (Isaiah 28:10, KJV)

Heaven builds steadily, not suddenly.

A believer becomes strong in whatever they do daily. Faith is no exception.

Abiding Turns Truth Into Instinct

When Jesus said, "Abide in Me," He was describing a lifestyle of returning again and again, not a burst of devotion, but a steady remaining. Abiding means continuing long enough for truth to become instinct rather than effort.

When you truly abide:

Your emotions no longer dictate your devotion.

Your discipline begins to outweigh your discouragement.

Your choices align with truth before your feelings follow.

Your confidence grows from Scripture rather than from your

mood.

Your faith stops depending on inspiration and begins resting on consistency.

Fruit grows where connection remains. Jesus made this clear:

> *"…He that abideth in me, and I in him, the same bringeth forth much fruit:"*
> (John 15:5, KJV)

Fruit is the result of connection over time, not the immediate achievement of perfection.

Elias learned this in his workshop. The first days were slow. Nothing looked different. But each small, repeated act created strength he could not see at first. Endurance turned a forgotten building into a place of purpose.

Endurance Is Built One Small Step at a Time

A single prayer may feel small. One act of obedience may feel invisible. A few minutes in Scripture may feel ordinary.

But God measures faithfulness, not size.

Every prayer whispered, every verse repeated, every moment of self-restraint, every decision to forgive, every time you open your Bible when you feel nothing at all; these become the steps that shape endurance.

This is why Scripture speaks of perseverance with such urgency:

> *"But he that shall endure unto the end, the same shall be saved."*
> (Matthew 24:13, KJV)

"…in due season we shall reap, if we faint not."
(Galatians 6:9, KJV)

"…be thou faithful unto death, and I will give thee a crown of life."
(Revelation 2:10, KJV)

Endurance is the bridge between seed and harvest. It is what turns hearing the Word of God into obedience that transforms the life.

Obedience Is Not Proved by What We Start, But by What We Sustain

Anyone can begin a race, but few continue when enthusiasm fades, and even fewer finish with joy.

Elias rebuilt the workshop not because he felt a surge of inspiration every morning, but because he was determined to obey the instruction God had given him. One board. One beam. One hour at a time. Each day strengthened the next.

Enduring obedience does not feel dramatic. But it is always supernatural.

God does not measure the greatness of your obedience by its visibility, but by its consistency. A few minutes of Scripture become insight, small prayers become breakthroughs, quiet faithfulness becomes visible fruit, simple obedience becomes supernatural outcomes, and daily choices become spiritual instincts.

Just like the vineyard's slow-growing vines, endurance transforms what looks ordinary into something overflowing with life. God uses repetition to deepen roots. Over time, those deep roots produce fruit that can withstand the weight of harvest.

Endurance Purifies Motivation

True endurance reveals why we obey. At first, we often obey because we feel inspired. A message moves us, conviction stirs us, and we respond in the strength of that moment. Over time, inspiration gives way to trust, and we continue because we believe God is faithful and His Word is true. But when obedience matures, it is no longer sustained merely by inspiration or even by trust alone. It is sustained by love. Enduring obedience grows until it becomes the expression of a heart that loves the One who commands.

Jesus said,

> *"If ye love me, keep my commandments"*
> (John 14:15, KJV)

Love sustains what excitement cannot. Love continues when feelings shift. Love obeys even when the reasons are not fully understood.

Elias reached that turning point. What began as a simple resolve matured into love. The rebuilding was no longer about restoring a building; it became about honoring the voice that called him to rise and build. And when obedience is rooted in love, endurance no longer feels heavy. It becomes joy.

The Enemy Fights Endurance More Than Inspiration

Satan rarely fights the beginning of a God-given assignment; he fights its continuation. He knows that inspiration often fades quickly, but endurance is what produces lasting fruit. If he can weaken your consistency, he can weaken your fruit, because fruit is formed through sustained obedience over time. This is why spiritual opposition often intensifies after obedience begins. The initial step may go unchallenged, but the steady return to that step, day after day, threatens far more. What begins with resolve must be guarded with perseverance, for the enemy seeks not merely to stop your start, but to erode your endurance.

Doubts multiply.

Fatigue rises.

Distractions intensify.

Progress feels slow.

Results appear delayed.

But this resistance is proof that your endurance is advancing into territory the enemy wants to keep barren.

> *"Submit yourselves therefore to God. Resist the devil, and he will flee from you."*
> (James 4:7, KJV)

Submission is obedience, resistance is endurance, and fleeing is the enemy's inevitable outcome. This is the progression of faith under pressure.

Endurance Is Not Grinding; It Is Grace Strengthening

Biblical endurance is not self-striving. It is dependence on God.

Scripture does not ask us to endure by willpower, but by grace:

> *"...be strong in the Lord, and in the power of his might."*
> (Ephesians 6:10, KJV)

Grace empowers what human strength cannot sustain. It makes obedience possible on the days when emotions are empty and strengthens the heart when progress is invisible. In moments of weariness, it lifts the arms of faith and carries the believer forward when personal resolve feels insufficient.

Endurance is not grinding your way through obedience. Endurance is cooperating with grace long enough to see what God promised.

The Reward of Endurance

God never wastes endurance.

> *"…ye have need of patience, that, after ye have done the will of God, ye might receive the promise."*
> (Hebrews 10:36, KJV)

The fulfillment of God's promises is often positioned behind long stretches of obedience. The promise is spoken beforehand, but endurance prepares the heart to receive its fulfillment.

When the workshop stood complete, Elias did not simply look at a finished building. He looked at a testimony shaped by days and weeks of returning to the same command: build.

It was not the structure itself that God honored, but the endurance that built it. The wood and stone were visible, but the faithfulness behind them was what carried weight in heaven. What stood before Elias was more than a finished workshop; it was the evidence of sustained obedience. God's pleasure was not in the completed form, but in the steadfast heart that returned to the work again and again until it was done.

Endurance Makes a Life Usable

In every believer God uses, one trait appears repeatedly:

They keep showing up.

Moses kept returning to Pharaoh. David kept returning to the place of worship. Daniel kept praying three times a day. The apostles kept preaching. Jesus Himself kept rising early to seek the Father.

Endurance makes a vessel usable. Not talent, not passion, not emotional highs, but endurance.

Elias learned this truth through every board lifted, every nail driven, and every day he returned to what God commanded. Endurance does not seek attention or draw notice; it simply remains. And it is through those who remain that God builds His kingdom.

Reflection and Practice

1. Reflection
Ask this honestly before the Lord: Where in my walk with God have I started well but grown inconsistent, and what does that reveal about what I truly trust in? Let Him bring specific areas to mind: time in the Word, prayer, a calling or assignment you once pursued, a relationship you were stewarding, or an act of service or generosity you once practiced faithfully. Is my obedience mostly tied to how I feel, or to who He is?

Write what comes to mind without editing it. This is not meant to cause you shame, but to bring you clarity.

2. Scripture Meditation

Read these passages aloud several times, slowly:

"This book of the law shall not depart out of thy mouth; but thou shalt meditate therein day and night, that thou mayest observe to do according to all that is written therein: for then thou shalt make thy way prosperous, and then thou shalt have good success."
(Joshua 1:8, KJV)

"…He that abideth in me, and I in him, the same bringeth forth much fruit: for without me ye can do nothing."
(John 15:5, KJV)

"And let us not be weary in well doing: for in due season we shall reap, if we faint not."
(Galatians 6:9, KJV)

Ask: What word or phrase stands out most today? What does this reveal about how God sees endurance? Sit quietly with that phrase for one full minute.

3. Prayer of Alignment

Lord, You see every place where I start strong and fade quickly. You know the promises I have made, the habits I have begun, the assignments I accepted, and the moments when I grew tired and let go. I confess that I have often relied on emotion rather than endurance, on inspiration rather than abiding. Today, I ask You to anchor me. Teach me not just to begin, but to remain. Plant in me a love for Your Word that outlasts my moods, a devotion that returns to You day and night, and a faithfulness that keeps showing up even when I feel nothing. I receive Your grace as my strength. I cannot endure by willpower, but I can endure by Your Spirit. Make obedience my instinct, not my occasional effort. In Jesus' name, amen.

4. Action Step

Establish one non-negotiable daily obedience, and protect it for seven days.

Ask the Holy Spirit, "Lord, what is one simple daily practice You are asking me to commit to in this season?"

It may be ten focused minutes in one passage, a set time of prayer, praying with your spouse or family, writing one page in a journal, or a nightly moment of thanksgiving.

Write this clearly: "By Your grace, Lord, for the next seven days I will…"

Choose a specific time and place. Endurance becomes easier when the when and where are already decided.

Keep this commitment as worship, not performance. If you miss a day, do not quit. Resume the next day. The victory is in returning, not in never stumbling.

5. Practice for the Week

For the next seven days, let this chapter move from principle to pattern.

Morning: Abide before you act. Pray, "Lord Jesus, today I choose to abide in You." Read Joshua 1:8 and John 15:5 aloud. Recommit to your one daily obedience.

Midday: Endurance checkpoint. Pause and ask, "Am I still walking in what God asked today, or have I drifted?" If scattered, pray, "Strengthen me with might by Your Spirit in the inner man," and take one small step of obedience.

Evening: Review with grace. Ask, "Where did I endure today? Where did I drift? What will endurance look like tomorrow?" Thank Him for every sign of faithfulness. Confess any drifting and recommit.

Repeat this rhythm for one full week. By week's end, obedience will feel more natural, emotions will have less control over devotion, and returning to God after a stumble will become quicker and easier. This is the beginning of endurance, where God turns quiet faithfulness into a life that lasts.

Closing Prayer

"Father, You have called me not only to believe, but to continue. Teach me to walk faithfully, to rise early and seek You, to hold Your Word close when the road feels long. Let obedience become my rhythm, endurance my strength, and peace my companion. May those who watch my steps see You reflected in the path I walk. In Jesus' name, Amen."

Chapter 12

The Fruit of Obedience

"But the fruit of the Spirit is love, joy, peace, longsuffering, gentleness, goodness, faith, meekness, temperance: against such there is no law. ... If we live in the Spirit, let us also walk in the Spirit."
(Galatians 5:22–25, KJV)

Autumn came quietly that year, slipping in on cool evenings and mornings touched with silver frost. The vineyard, once bursting with green abundance, now wore a noble stillness. Leaves blushed gold and crimson at the edges. Clusters of grapes, heavy with the fullness of the season, hung like dark jewels beneath the fading light.

The land itself seemed to exhale. The restless energy of summer faded into a slower rhythm. Wind moved gently through the valley, no longer sharp with storms but thoughtful, as though even the air had learned patience.

Elias walked slowly through the rows, savoring the hush that comes when a harvest is nearly complete. Each vine seemed to bow under its own blessing, as if acknowledging the One who had brought fruit from furrow and faith.

The silence was not empty. It carried memory.

He remembered seasons when these same rows had been thin and uncertain, when the vines clung to life instead of bearing fruit. Now the branches leaned heavily with abundance. What had once required desperate prayer now invited grateful stewardship.

He paused near the center of the vineyard, where the first seed of obedience had once been sown. He pressed his palm against a vine that had nearly withered years ago. Now it stood strong, its branches thick, its fruit abundant. He whispered a quiet prayer of thanks, remembering what it had cost to reach this season.

Memory rose in fragments. The famine. The rebuilding. The long evenings when hope felt fragile. The quiet whisper that had first called him to obedience when no fruit yet existed to justify the effort. Those days felt distant now, yet their imprint remained written across the vineyard like an invisible testimony.

The workshop stood behind him like a sentinel of testimony. Its beams were now darkened by smoke and years of labor. Its shelves were full, its doors open to neighbors, strangers, and travelers who passed through the region. Many had been fed there. Many had rested. Many had prayed within its walls.

What had begun as a simple act of obedience had become a place where stories gathered. People came with burdens and left with quiet strength. Some returned simply to sit by the fire, letting the stillness restore something in them that the world had worn thin.

Hannah walked out to join him, a shawl draped across her shoulders. The wind tugged at the edges of her hair as she approached.

"Beautiful, isn't it?" she said, smiling at the rows.

Elias nodded. "It is more than I expected. More than I imagined the day we started."

"Obedience bears fruit," she said softly. "Always."

He reached for her hand, lifting it gently to his lips. "Not just in the vineyard. In us."

They stood together for a moment longer, letting the quiet of the field settle around them. It was the kind of silence that only follows seasons of perseverance. Not empty. Fulfilled.

They walked together toward the old fig tree near the edge of the property. Micah and Jonah were already there, gathering the last of the figs into baskets. Their laughter echoed across the field, mingling with the rustle of leaves and the distant call of migrating geese.

"Father," Micah called, holding up a full basket, "the tree gave more this year than any before."

Jonah grinned. "It is almost like it knows the Lord blessed us."

Elias smiled warmly. "It knows because creation listens. Fruit grows where God has touched the soil."

The boys returned to their work, gently lifting figs into the baskets so the skins would not bruise. Elias watched them carefully. They moved differently now than they had years ago. Their steps carried responsibility. Their laughter carried maturity.

As they worked, the sun dipped lower, turning the hills into rolling waves of amber. Hannah brushed a curl behind Jonah's ear and said, "Do you know why God gives seasons of abundance?"

Jonah shrugged. "Because He loves us?"

"Yes," she said, "but there is more."

Micah leaned in. "Tell us."

Hannah knelt between them. "Fruit is never the end of a story. It is the beginning of responsibility. When God blesses you, He is calling you to steward what He has multiplied."

Elias nodded thoughtfully. "And to prepare for what comes next."

Jonah frowned. "Next? After the harvest?"

Elias glanced over the vineyard. "A vineyard that bears fruit must still be pruned. Growth always invites another season of shaping."

Micah exhaled slowly. "So even when everything is good, God still works on us?"

"Especially then," Elias said gently. "Blessing is the most delicate season for the human heart. It can make a man careless or proud if he forgets where his strength comes from."

Hannah rested a hand on his arm. "But if a heart stays humble, blessing becomes fuel for what God will do next."

The boys let the words sink in as they gathered the last figs and carried the baskets toward the house. The sky deepened into a purple haze, stars blinking into existence like lanterns hung in heaven.

A cool wind moved across the vineyard, lifting the scent of crushed leaves and ripened fruit. The season felt complete yet unfinished. Elias recognized the feeling well. It was the quiet space between gratitude and preparation.

Later that night, the family sat by the fire inside the workshop. The warmth of the flames flickered across the walls, casting a soft glow on every beam. The scent of roasted figs and bread filled the air.

Elias closed his eyes, letting the sounds of his family settle around him. The crackle of wood. Jonah's soft humming. Hannah's quiet prayers rising and falling like breath.

The workshop had become more than a shelter. It was a living room for the work of God. Within its walls, laughter had been restored, grief had softened, and weary travelers had rediscovered hope.

For the first time in a long while, he felt completely present. Completely at peace.

Peace, however, did not mean stillness. Elias had learned that the Spirit often speaks most clearly when the soul has grown quiet enough to listen.

Then, without warning, a stirring rose in his spirit. It was not fear. It was not trouble. It was the same quiet prompting he had felt years ago, the day the Shepherd visited him in the dream. It carried weight. It carried wisdom. It carried a warning.

His eyes opened slowly.

Hannah noticed first. "What is it?" she whispered.

Elias looked at the fire, watching the flames curl and lean as though responding to an unseen wind.

"The fruit has come," he said softly. "The season has changed."

Hannah's eyes narrowed. "Changed how?"

Elias swallowed, his voice low. "The harvest always invites a new kind of battle."

Micah sat up straighter. "A battle?"

Jonah's eyes widened. "Father, what do you mean?"

Elias took a long breath before answering.

"There is a war that follows every season of blessing. Not against flesh or blood, but inside us. A war between the spirit that longs for God and the flesh that longs for comfort."

The workshop fell silent.

Hannah placed her hand over his.

"You feel it, too," she said quietly.

Elias nodded. "God grew fruit in us so He could grow more through us. But the next season will test what we have become."

He looked at his sons, his voice steady and warm.

"The true fruit of obedience is not the grapes in the vineyard. It is the heart that can endure the pruning that comes after."

Jonah whispered, "So what happens now?"

Elias stood, stirring the fire with a single stroke. Sparks rose like tiny stars.

"Now," he said, "we prepare our hearts for the journey to come. The Lord will teach us how to walk in the Spirit, and not the flesh."

The flames brightened, their light catching the cedar beams above them.

Outside, beyond the vineyard, the wind shifted.

Something unseen was moving.

Something that would call them deeper.

Something that would test everything they had learned.

And the next chapter of their walk with God began before any of them spoke another word.

The Fruit That Follows Faithfulness

Fruit is not the finish line of a believer's journey. In Scripture, seasons of fruit are often followed by pruning, stretching, or sending. God does not give a harvest so that we can settle into comfort. He gives harvest so that we can grow into the next assignment He intends.

"Herein is my Father glorified, that ye bear much fruit;"
(John 15:8, KJV)

But earlier in the chapter, Jesus teaches a sobering companion truth: Fruit requires pruning.

"…every branch that beareth fruit, he purgeth it, that it may bring forth more fruit."
(John 15:2, KJV)

Pruning is not punishment. Pruning is preparation. Pruning is proof that the branch is alive.

In Elias's story, the vineyard moved into a season of fullness. The workshop was restored. Peace rested in the home. Obedience had produced visible fruit. Yet even in that season, Elias told his sons that full branches must be trimmed. He understood the Heavenly Gardener's wisdom. Fullness is not the end of growth. Even fruitful branches must be pruned.

This pattern is woven throughout Scripture.

Blessing Requires Stewardship

God never gives increase without responsibility. Blessing is a trust, not a trophy.

When God placed Adam in a full garden, He commanded him to dress it and keep it.

"And the Lord God took the man, and put him into the garden of Eden to dress it and to keep it."
(Genesis 2:15, KJV)

Abundance requires tending.

When Israel entered a land flowing with milk and honey, God warned them not to forget the Lord or to neglect His commandments.

"Beware that thou forget not the Lord thy God, in not keeping his commandments, and his judgments, and his statutes, which I command thee this day."
(Deuteronomy 8:11, KJV)

Blessing requires obedience.

When Jesus multiplied the loaves and fishes, the disciples were told to gather the fragments.

"When they were filled, he said unto his disciples, Gather up the fragments that remain, that nothing be lost."
(John 6:12, KJV)

Nothing God provides is meant to be wasted.

Fruit comes with instructions. Harvest comes with responsibility. Blessing comes with stewardship.

In the same way, Elias did not stand still once the vineyard flourished. He walked the rows. He tested the weight of the grapes. He taught his sons how to care for what God had increased. When God gives fruit, He also gives the call to guard it.

Blessing Requires Discernment

Fruit does not signal that you have arrived.

Fruit signals that you are ready for greater responsibility.

Many believers mistake the feeling of success for the end of their labor. Yet throughout Scripture, blessing often signals the beginning of greater responsibility.

After David became king, God immediately led him into new battles.

"And David inquired of the Lord, saying, Shall I go up to the Philistines? wilt thou deliver them into mine hand? And the Lord said unto David, Go up: for I will doubtless deliver the Philistines into thine hand."
(2 Samuel 5:19, KJV)

After Joseph rose to power, God used him to preserve nations, not merely to enjoy authority.

"And all countries came into Egypt to Joseph for to buy corn; because that the famine was so sore in all lands."
(Genesis 41:57, KJV)

After Solomon dedicated the Temple, God warned him to walk carefully so the blessing would remain.

"And if thou wilt walk before me, as David thy father walked, in integrity of heart, and in uprightness, to do according to all that I have commanded thee, and wilt keep my statutes and my judgments:"
(1 Kings 9:4, KJV)

Blessing does not relieve us of the need for discernment. Blessing increases the need for discernment.

Once the workshop in Elias's story was built, a shift happened again. The peace was real, but it was not final. Fullness did not signal rest. It signaled readiness. Something new was approaching. And his spirit sensed it.

This is the nature of fruit: it invites examination. What is God pruning? What must be released? What must be strengthened for the next season?

The Father trims not only what is dead but also what is good so that it may become greater.

Blessing Requires Seeking

Fruit should not make us complacent. Fruit should make us hungry.

Throughout the Bible, God's servants sought Him again after harvest moments.

After Elijah called fire down on Mount Carmel, he fled into the wilderness and journeyed to the mountain of God, where he sought the Lord's voice.

"And he arose, and did eat and drink, and went in the strength of that meat forty days and forty nights unto Horeb the mount of God."
(1 Kings 19:8, KJV)

After Peter hauled in a miraculous catch of fish, he fell at Jesus' feet and left everything to follow Him.

"And when they had brought their ships to land, they forsook all, and followed him."
(Luke 5:11, KJV)

After a season of successful church planting, Paul received fresh direction from the Lord through a vision.

"And a vision appeared to Paul in the night; There stood a man of Macedonia, and prayed him, saying, Come over into Macedonia, and help us."
(Acts 16:9, KJV)

Harvest is a holy summons. Success should never silence our need for God. Blessing should draw us closer, not lull us into drifting.

Elias's heart mirrored this pattern. When the vineyard reached fullness, he did not assume the season was complete. Something stirred within him. God was shifting the atmosphere again. Blessing had prepared him for deeper seeking.

Blessing Requires Readiness for the Next Assignment

Whenever God completes one season, He begins preparing the heart for the next.

When Elisha witnessed Elijah being taken up, he did not settle into the moment. Instead, he asked boldly for a double portion.

"And it came to pass, when they were gone over, that Elijah said unto Elisha, Ask what I shall do for thee, before I be taken away from thee. And Elisha said, I pray thee, let a double portion of thy spirit be upon me."
(2 Kings 2:9, KJV)

When the disciples saw the risen Christ, Jesus did not allow them to retreat into celebration, but commissioned them to preach the gospel to the entire world.

"And he said unto them, Go ye into all the world, and preach the gospel to every creature."
(Mark 16:15, KJV)

When Joshua entered the Promised Land, God commanded him to be strong and very courageous, reminding him that the fulfillment of promise still required faithful obedience.

"Only be thou strong and very courageous, that thou mayest observe to do according to all the law, which Moses my servant commanded thee: turn not from it to the right hand or to the left, that thou mayest prosper whithersoever thou goest."
(Joshua 1:7, KJV)

Fruit is preparation. Fruit is a launch pad. Fruit is God's invitation to greater stewardship.

So when Elias looked across a thriving vineyard and felt the wind shift, he was not sensing danger. He was sensing a calling.

God speaks to the heart in seasons of blessing because faith has been strengthened enough to receive bigger assignments.

Blessing Requires Endurance

"But the fruit of the Spirit is love, joy, peace, longsuffering, gentleness, goodness, faith, meekness, temperance:"
(Galatians 5:22–23, KJV)

This fruit grows on branches that remain. Fruitfulness is the reward of abiding, repenting, listening, obeying, and enduring. The work of the Spirit unfolds over time, often quietly and gradually, as the believer continues to walk faithfully with God. Each act of obedience, each return to the Lord after failure, and each moment of surrender becomes another step in the process through which spiritual fruit is formed.

Because this growth takes time, the believer must learn not to grow weary in the process. The harvest of spiritual fruit does not appear overnight, but it comes to those who continue faithfully in the path God has set before them. The life that keeps sowing obedience will eventually reap the fruit that God has promised.

That is why Paul wrote:

"And let us not be weary in well doing: for in due season we shall reap, if we faint not."
(Galatians 6:9, KJV)

Endurance keeps the soil alive in seasons of fruit and protects the harvest. It also prepares the branches for greater yield.

Blessing Is the Platform for Multiplication

In Scripture, blessing is never the final chapter. It is always the opening chapter of greater responsibility. When God entrusts someone with provision, favor, or increase, it is not meant to become a place of comfort or complacency. It is an invitation to steward what has been given with greater faithfulness. The blessing itself becomes the platform for the next assignment.

Throughout the Bible, those who received from God were also called to rise into deeper obedience. What God provided was not an end in itself, but preparation for what He intended to do next. Increase was meant to be managed, influence was meant to be used, and provision was meant to serve a purpose beyond personal gain.

In this way, blessing becomes both a gift and a responsibility. It calls the believer to remain humble, attentive, and ready for whatever God asks next. What begins as a reward for faithfulness quickly becomes an opportunity to demonstrate even greater faithfulness in the seasons that follow.

In Matthew, the servants who multiplied their talents were entrusted with more, and their master commended them for their faithfulness.

"His lord said unto him, Well done, thou good and faithful servant: thou hast been faithful over a few things, I will make thee ruler over many things: enter thou into the joy of thy lord."
(Matthew 25:21, KJV)

In Luke, Jesus filled Simon Peter's boat with fish, and then called him to leave his nets and become a fisher of men.

"And so was also James, and John, the sons of Zebedee, which were partners with Simon. And Jesus said unto Simon, Fear not; from henceforth thou shalt catch men."
(Luke 5:10, KJV)

In Job, God restored Job's losses and gave him twice as much as he had before.

"And the Lord turned the captivity of Job, when he prayed for his friends: also the Lord gave Job twice as much as he had before."
(Job 42:10, KJV)

After Elijah was taken up, Elisha received Elijah's mantle, and the Lord used him mightily in the ministry that followed.

"And when the sons of the prophets which were to view at Jericho saw him, they said, The spirit of Elijah doth rest on Elisha. And they came to meet him, and bowed themselves to the ground before him."
(2 Kings 2:15, KJV)

Multiplication follows faithfulness. Faithfulness follows obedience. Obedience follows revelation. Revelation follows seeking.

Elias experienced this spiritual pattern. As he overlooked the vineyard, he knew that the fruit was not the end. It was evidence that

God had been with him, and a sign that God was preparing him for what came next.

Blessing Is a Sign, Not a Destination

As God blesses us with a harvest, we must seek Him all the more carefully. Blessing is a sign that God has been faithful, and pruning is often a sign that He is preparing more. When seasons shift, it is often because God is calling His people into deeper obedience.

Fruit is not the end of obedience, but the beginning of greater stewardship. The blessings of God must be stewarded, His voice must be sought again, and the next assignment must be embraced. Through it all, the heart must remain tender, and the life fully surrendered.

You do not stop seeking God in the season of fruit. You seek Him more deeply. You listen more carefully. You examine more humbly.

And like Elisha beneath the falling mantle, you lift your hands and pray:

"Lord, what is the next portion You want me to carry?"

Reflection and Practice

1. Reflection

Ask the Lord honestly: What has God grown in my life in this season, and how am I stewarding that fruit for His purposes rather than my comfort? Let Him bring specifics to mind: a change in character, a breakthrough in your family, provision in work or finances, or growth in your calling, ministry, or business. Then ask a second question: Where might God be gently pruning or shifting me so that this fruit can multiply and not stagnate? Write whatever comes to mind without editing. This is not a performance review. It is a conversation with your Gardener.

2. Scripture Meditation

Read these passages aloud slowly, pausing between each one:

"Every branch in me that beareth not fruit he taketh away: and every branch that beareth fruit, he purgeth it, that it may bring forth more fruit."
(John 15:2, KJV)

"Herein is my Father glorified, that ye bear much fruit; so shall ye be my disciples."
(John 15:8, KJV)

"And let us not be weary in well doing: for in due season we shall reap, if we faint not."
(Galatians 6:9, KJV)

Ask: What phrase stands out most today? Is God speaking to me more about pruning, fruit, or not fainting? Sit with that phrase for a full minute and let it settle like rain on the soil of your heart.

3. Prayer of Alignment

Father, thank You for every trace of fruit You have grown in my life. Whatever love, joy, peace, or faithfulness I see in me, I know it is Your work. I confess that I have often treated blessings as destinations rather than as platforms for the next assignment. At times, I have loved comfort more than I have loved calling. Today I yield afresh to Your pruning.

Cut away what drains strength, even if it once seemed useful. Trim what is overgrown so that more of your life can flow through me. Do not let me become complacent in seasons of fruit. Teach me to seek You deeper when things are going well. Show me how to steward what You have given so that nothing You have grown in me is wasted. Prepare my heart for what You are entrusting to me next. In Jesus' name, amen.

4. Action Step

Set aside one focused hour this week for a "fruit and pruning review" with the Lord.

List the fruit. Write three headings:

What God Has Done in Me

What God Has Done for Me

What God Has Done through Me.

List specific examples from this season, even if they seem small.

Ask about stewardship. Next to each item, write, "How am I stewarding this fruit?" Are you protecting it, sharing it, growing it, or neglecting it?

Invite pruning. Pray, "Lord, in light of this fruit, what are You pruning right now? What are you asking me to release, adjust, or lay down so that this can multiply?" Write whatever He brings to mind. This page becomes a roadmap for your next steps.

5. Practice for the Week

Live this week as someone in a fruitful season that God is preparing to multiply.

Morning: Thank and AskPray, "Father, thank You for the fruit You have grown in my life. Show me how to steward it today." Read (John 15:2) and (John 15:8) aloud. Ask God to guide you in one small act of stewardship.

Midday: Discern the Shift Pause and ask, "Am I using today's blessing to draw closer to God, or to drift into comfort?" If you sense pruning, whisper, "Lord, I receive Your pruning as preparation. Help me cooperate."

Evening: Offer the Fruit Back Review your day with God. Where did I see even a small measure of the Spirit's fruit? Where did I ignore or mishandle something God is growing? Thank Him for every sign of His work. Confess any areas where you have neglected what He entrusted to you. Pray, "Lord, everything You have grown in me today, I give back to You. Use it and increase it."

Repeat this rhythm for seven days. By week's end, you will see fruit not as a finish line but as the beginning of multiplication.

Closing Prayer

"Father, You are the Gardener of my soul. Thank You for every season for planting, pruning, and producing fruit in me. Help me to remain in You, to welcome Your hand even when it cuts, and to bear the kind of fruit that glorifies Your name. Let the peace of Your Spiritfill the house of my heart until it overflows. May my life prove the power of obedience and the beauty of surrender. In Jesus' name, Amen."

Closing

A WORD BEFORE WE PART

My journey with God did not begin when I became an adult or when I started writing this book. It began when I was a boy of about ten, when I first started having dreams from God. At the time, I did not understand what they meant. I only knew that something in me was sensitive to the voice of God long before I had the maturity to recognize it.

I grew up in a broken Christian home. We attended church regularly, and I always considered myself a follower of Jesus Christ. Even so, my understanding of Him was incomplete. I believed that if I prayed for something and it did not appear miraculously, then God's answer was, "No, I do not want you to have that." I quietly assumed that God moved only in sudden supernatural moments rather than through relationship, stewardship, and obedience.

This misunderstanding reached into every part of my life, including my relationship with money. I believed that being generous meant giving everything away and denying myself any blessing. I thought that taking care of myself financially was wrong and that being a good Christian meant giving even what I did not have.

Over time, I learned a complicated but necessary truth. Generosity is from God. Neglecting yourself is not. God did not call me to live empty, but to be a faithful steward who can bless others without living in lack.

Everything began to change in my late thirties when I started seeking God with a different posture. I began resisting the things of the flesh and studying the Scriptures with purpose. I questioned the teachings I had accepted that did not line up with God's Word. I started recording my dreams and visions and comparing them to Scripture instead of to my emotions. I listened to sermons from teachers across the body of Christ. I read books, listened to podcasts, and prayed with intention. I was on a mission to understand the God I believed in, not only through tradition but through truth.

That mission changed my life.

As I began asking God for what aligned with His will rather than my own desires, I experienced genuine spiritual growth, and my understanding of who God is deepened. My relationship with Him deepened. The spiritual hunger that was awakened in that season has never faded. If anything, it has increased. Every step I have taken toward God has revealed more of His heart than I knew in my childhood or early adulthood.

I share this not because my story is unusual but because it is genuine. God took a young boy who dreamed, a grown man who misunderstood Him, and a seeker who was willing to begin again, and He started to teach me who He truly is. This book is part of that story. These chapters are not theories. They are the result of years spent asking, listening, adjusting, and surrendering.

My prayer is that as you come to the end of this book, something in you is stirred with the same hunger God placed in me. A desire to know Him not through assumption but through relationship. Not through fear but through truth. Not through distant belief but through daily obedience.

If God could take my misunderstandings, my broken beginnings, and my incomplete theology and shape them into a deeper walk with Him, then He can do the same for you. He is faithful to all who seek Him, and He rewards those who pursue Him with an honest heart.

May your journey with God continue long after these pages. May your hunger grow, your understanding deepen, and your relationship with Him become more real than ever. God has been pursuing you long before you learned to pursue Him.

Now I pray this over you. In the mighty name of Jesus!

"The Lord bless thee, and keep thee: The Lord make his face shine upon thee, and be gracious unto thee: The Lord lift up his countenance upon thee, and give thee peace."
(Numbers 6:24–26, KJV)